THE
ECLIPSE
OF
CITIZENSHIP:
Power and Participation in Contemporary Politics

THE ECLIPSE
OF CITIZENSHIP
Power and Participation
in Contemporary Politics

ROBERT J. PRANGER

University of Kentucky

HOLT, RINEHART AND WINSTON, INC.

New York   Chicago   San Francisco   Atlanta   Dallas
Montreal   Toronto   London

Copyright © 1968 by Holt, Rinehart and Winston, Inc.

All rights reserved

Library of Congress Catalog Card Number: 68-21784

SBN Number   03-069665-8

Printed in the United States of America

90123   13   9876543

For my children

Preface

This book is written to stimulate thought about citizenship as an important political status now in eclipse. I am presenting a case for a view of politics that takes into account the participation of citizens as an enterprise with values and distinctive forms of action separate from the more ordinary struggle for power and authority usually associated with politics. My argument is conditional in that it depends on a number of assumptions, definitions, and conclusions which limit the discussion. Generalizations are made within the context of these limits. In this discussion I have paid little attention to the law of citizenship. Instead, my attempt is to think about citizenship, the politics of power and the politics of participation, the causes of frustration among citizens, and the psychological background and cultural setting in which citizens as active participators may develop. *The Eclipse of Citizenship* is not the last word on these subjects, but I hope that for readers it will be a step in the direction of increased awareness.

For his interest in this essay, I would like to thank Professor Sheldon S. Wolin, of the University of California at Berkeley. Financial support for this essay has been provided by the University of Illinois Research Board and by the Kentucky Research Foundation, and their assistance is gratefully acknowledged.

Lexington, Ky.   R. J. P.
April 1968

Contents

THE
ECLIPSE
OF
CITIZENSHIP:
Power and Participation in Contemporary Politics

Introduction

In an important essay the social psychologist Kurt Lewin once contrasted three types of group dynamics, "authoritarian," "democratic," and "laissez faire" (or anarchistic). His main points in this contrast emphasized that democratic groups do have government, and therefore should not be confused with anarchy, but that the governments of democratic groups move by sentiments emanating from each group as a whole and translate these sentiments into a leadership structure more open to, and conditioned by, all the group members than in authoritarian situations.[1]*

This work by Lewin proved seminal. Among other developments, it influenced the profound analysis of relationships between political personality and group contexts in the now-famous "authoritarian personality" studies. Of interest to the present essay, however, is Lewin's notion that between authoritarian order, with its pressure toward discipline passed downward from elites to nonelites, and anarchism, with no discipline or order at all, lies democracy with its emphasis on both leadership and common undertakings sponsored by wide civic participation. In this age of ultimate international violence, interminable cold war, and universal

---

* The notes for the references in the text appear at the end of each chapter throughout the book.

civil strife, this argument of Lewin's should be recalled and reinforced.

Violence represents the end product drawn from erasing the buffer zones between hierarchical authority and anarchy to such an extent that the alternative to political order becomes no order at all. In the domestic political sphere the masses revolt against the few because, among other reasons, the masses have no real control over their destinies. The few must perish, along with their real and imagined intimates, so that the many may really live for the first time. Conversely, the autocratic regime rules by violence: "government by flogging," as one observer has described ancient Oriental empires,[2] or government by "terror," as others have labelled modern totalitarianism.[3] On the international scene the juxtaposition of autocracy and anarchy is even more pronounced: Absolutely sovereign states relate to each other in contexts where buffer zones sometimes exist (international bodies, regional arrangements, and the like), but these zones have very limited control over the conduct of states.[4] Out of such stark contrasts between high and low, absolute authority and no authority at all, come not only the wars and revolutions which represent the main antitheses to politics,[5] but also that feverish violence associated with contemporary urban life.

Alternatives to authoritarian power and anarchistic impotence ought to be welcomed, therefore, as means for preserving politics—the method by which men artificially order existence so as to have a good life—as well as peace. The notion of politics as an artificial ordering of life for purposes of higher values as well as for sheer physical survival will be more thoroughly explored in the pages to follow. Such a view of politics seems utopian, and to some extent it is, if by "utopian" we mean an emphasis on political potentials as contrasted with political realities. This is an essay on both realities and potentials. At the same time, its approach is prescriptive as well as descriptive, as noted below. The prescription is both ideal (in the sense of moral or "normative") and clinical (in the sense of good or better political "health").

In preserving a humanized politics and the associated value of peace, citizenship—the most basic political status—will also benefit. The ordinary citizen prospers more than anyone else in Lewin's democratic group dynamics: By participating in politics in such a way that he actually enjoys power and creates a commonwealth, the citizen has something important to do. He becomes worthwhile rather than worthless, and this swells his sense of authenticity while assuaging his anxieties about political order. Both state and citizen prosper through such participation.

While Lewin labels the alternative to authoritarianism and anarchy "democracy," this last form of group politics will be called "participation" here. (In contrast to participation, there persists another type of politics, "power.") Both substantive and methodological justifications can be made for this shift in terms.

First, there is a substantive reason why it proves necessary to substitute "participation" for what Lewin means by "democracy." Democracy, as most use the term today in political science, means elite governance with periodic election ceremonials by a populace who determine, among competing leaders and their coalitions, who shall govern. Since democracy is pluralistic, between elections various minorities rule, in nonrandomized order, according to various issues raised in the political system. Most political scientists would accept this description abbreviated from the writings of Robert A. Dahl,[6] a description appropriately labelled "the elitist theory of democracy."[7] Such a picture of democracy has little resemblance to Lewin's group-dynamics model of a self-starting leadership, instituted by the common membership of the group and deferring to that membership. Perhaps the difference in definitions can be traced to the smallness of Lewin's experimental groups as contrasted with the immensity of today's political units, though it will be argued otherwise in this essay.[8]

What is important for the substantive contrast used here between "power" and "participation," however, is that democracy is not only identified with power, but increasingly shares many of the characteristics of authoritarian power. It shares them to such an extent that certain kinds of typically democratic values, such as individual dignity and liberal education, become more and more purely mythical, contrived, and tenuous in the world of real action. Thus the contrast between power—meaning hierarchical dominance—and participation—meaning group undertakings which not only involve a common membership but rely on this membership to initiate and direct those undertakings—seems more meaningful. Power, it will be argued in the following pages, has won the day, participation has lost. The citizen, whose chief duty is to participate, is disappearing as an important political actor. The result represents the evaporation not only of a central political status (which means in turn a decline of politics in favor of efficient, instrumental organization) but also the loss of certain key political values which can be sustained in practice only where there is someone to practice them.

Second, in methodological terms, power and participation can be used as "ideal types" without running the risk of overloading either with value connotations.[9] Obviously, I prefer a redress of balance between power and participation; I "value" participation. But democracy has for so long been a "hurrah word," associated with a popular sovereignty which nowhere exists, that it is now useless as a descriptive term for meaningful civic participation. Modern democracy, defined as a common government by the whole membership, constitutes a mythical conception appropriately confined to the same cage with other political dragons and unicorns.

On the other hand, democracy can be realistically discussed as a form of power politics. As now practiced, democracy is a species of power, not of participation. To fill the theoretical gap in political theory left by democracy's passage to power—and democracy was once identified, at least in political theory, more with participation—there is needed a term other than power. This essay is content with "participation" and will seek to define this form of politics and contrast it with "power." *Why* political theory—at least a political theory pretending to relate to experience—needs any longer to deal with participation, represents a question that is reserved for later treatment.

The problem of dealing with contemporary citizenship, then, is to find a language of analysis capable of coping with citizenship in terms dynamic enough to assess changes in the ideal and practice of civic participation, or in what some have called "civic virtue." Hopefully, the ideas developed in the following pages meet these requirements. At the same time that assessment, definition, and description are taking place, however, prescription follows close behind.[10] This essay concludes with some suggestions of the means for changing the current imbalance between power and participation so that participation may prosper. It is hoped that this presentation will make a contribution not only to clearer understanding of a contemporary political problem but also to keener thinking about how one might proceed, in thinking and acting, to institute political change.

The following essay presents a kind of "citizen's view of politics." After much thought on the subject of citizenship, it is my opinion that what is ordinarily called "politics" is actually "power politics"—the activities of leaders, activists, and influentials in the public marketplace. Contrasted to this form of politics is another, the politics of citizenship or "participatory politics." In the latter political form, questions arise of direct relevance to the ordinary citizen. On the one hand are issues of leadership, such as competition and compromise. But there also exist political questions, such as personal freedom and community, that are of central concern to citizens who must live within the political order and who do not have any special advantages regarding decisions made within that order. In other words, there seem to be two politics, called here the politics of power and the politics of participation, instead of one political order. Obviously there is considerable overlapping, yet the differences between the political forms appear, at least to me, both interesting and significant enough that I place them in two distinct categories. This dualism conforms to one of the central truths about the symbolic meaning of language: The essence of meaning, in Susanne K. Langer's words, "lies in the realm of logic, where one does not deal with qualities, but only with relations."[11] The definition of politics will clearly vary from culture to culture, and within each culture it will vary from one type of political actor to another. To paraphrase a New Testament admonition, ordinary citizens may be "in" the world of power but not "of" it. Conversely, leaders may also be nominal citizens, but their positions prevent them from being "of" the citizenry.

Notes to the Introduction

1. Kurt Lewin, "The Practicality of Democracy," in William Ebenstein, ed., *Modern Political Thought, The Great Issues*, 2d ed. (New York: Holt, Rinehart and Winston, Inc., 1960), pp. 91–99.

2. Karl Wittfogel, *Oriental Despotism* (New Haven, Conn.: Yale University Press, 1957), p. 143.

3. See Hannah Arendt's discussion of "terror" in totalitarianism, *The Origins of Totalitarianism*, 2d ed. (New York: Meridian Books, Inc., 1958), chapter 13.

4. Note the discussion of European unity in Ernest B. Haas, *Beyond the Nation-State* (Stanford, Calif.: Stanford University Press, 1964).

5. The apolitical tendencies of revolution and war are noted in Hannah Arendt, *On Revolution* (London: Faber & Faber, Ltd., 1963), chapter 1. Both revolution and war tend toward the "domain of violence," which is antipolitical to the extent that it rules.

6. See Robert A. Dahl's *A Preface to Democratic Theory* (Chicago: University of Chicago Press, 1956) and *Who Governs?* (New Haven, Conn.: Yale University Press, 1961).

7. See Jack L. Walker, "A Critique of the Elitist Theory of Democracy," pp. 285–295, and Dahl, "Further Reflections on 'The Elitist Theory of Democracy,'" pp. 296–305, *American Political Science Review*, Vol. LX (June 1966). Peter Bachrach, *The Theory of Democracy Elitism, A Critique* (Boston: Little, Brown & Company, 1967).

8. Dahl adheres to the thesis that immensity does make a difference but attempts to find alternative forms of contemporary democracy in his "The City in the Future of Democracy," *American Political Science Review*, LXI (December 1967), 953–970.

9. For an explanation of "ideal type," see Max Weber, "Objectivity in Social Science and Social Policy" (1904), in *Max Weber on the Methodology of the Social Sciences*, trans. and ed. by Edward A. Shils and Henry A. Finch (New York: The Free Press, 1949), pp. 90–112.

10. On the distinction between description and prescription in political theory, see Thomas P. Jenkin, *The Study of Political Theory* (New York: Random House, Inc., 1955), pp. 1–4.

11. Susanne K. Langer, *Philosophy in a New Key* (New York: New American Library of World Literature, 1958), p. 56.

Chapter 1

THE POLITICAL MAN (HOMO POLITICUS) IS ONE WHO DEMANDS THE MAXIMIZATION OF HIS POWER IN RELATION TO ALL HIS VALUES, WHO EXPECTS POWER TO DETERMINE POWER, AND WHO IDENTIFIES WITH OTHERS AS A MEANS OF ENHANCING POWER POSITION AND POTENTIAL.

Harold D. Lasswell and Abraham Kaplan
Power and Society

CITIZENSHIP. . . MEANS THE CONTRIBUTION OF OUR INSTRUCTED JUDGMENT TO THE COMMON GOOD. IT MAY LEAD US TO SUPPORT THE STATE; BUT IT MAY LEAD US ALSO TO OPPOSE IT.

Harold J. Laski
A Grammar of Politics

1

The Two Politics: Participation and Power

Definitions provide means for drawing boundaries around subject areas, thus establishing certain conventional limits for the direction of inquiry. Since this essay is mainly concerned with national citizenship, it seems important for the analysis that follows to begin by bringing the central topic into focus: National citizenship may be defined as basic membership in a nation state—a status which gives the occupants freedom in the sense that they are full members with special rights and duties denied to others. This status is highly prized. Chief Justice Earl Warren of the United States Supreme Court thinks citizenship so important that he has called it "the right to have rights" and condemns its punitive withdrawal from individuals as "a cruel and unusual punishment."[1] Literally, citizenship means official identity, as basic and important as one's personal name; in fact, a good deal more important, for having a name without a citizenship deprives a person of that identity by which most of the world judges him. To be "Jim Smith" with no citizenship makes a man less human today than being "Jim Smith, American." As Americans who decide to live in self-imposed exile discover, no matter what their race, creed, or color, they continue to be viewed as Americans by their newly adopted country. It is only a slight exaggeration to say that if those without national political affiliation seem, in the eyes of international relations, less human than those with such affiliation, then "man" becomes "human" in the fullest sense only through his citizenship. For those who value more ecumenical loyalties than the modern national state—the brotherhood of all men regardless of national origin, for instance—Jim Smith may rank as important as Jim Smith, American. But at this point the question is not what ought to be, only what is the case. Agreeable or not, the fact remains that national citizenship gives official identity, and without official identity one becomes less human than with such identity. In the language of psychology, citizenship supplies an integral segment of one's "identity pattern," something taken as second nature.[2]

Used in the above sense, citizenship is a universalist definition applying to all specific practices. Like all such definitions, however, this one has a limitation. What any universalist term or any practice suggested by that term will mean, varies to some extent with the context in which it appears. Citizenship is legal membership, not just in any state, but in *a* state. One usually speaks of *American* citizens, *French* citizens, and *Indian* citizens, not about citizens in general. Again, those who share more cosmopolitan sympathies than national ones might refer to a *European* or a *World* citizenship, but very likely they have in mind a specific European or World organization with a basic membership. How can one say anything meaningful about citizenship in general, as this essay aims to do? And what importance attaches to such general statements, even if they are made? What citizenship is involved? Austrian? Yemeni? Australian? Japanese?

GENERALIZATIONS
ABOUT CONTEMPORARY CITIZENSHIP

Certain general and important statements *can* be made about modern citizenship. These generalizations relate to what appears to be a central political problem of contemporary life, the balance between the politics of participation and the politics of power. This balance now tilts far in the direction of hierarchical power, and unless it can be redressed in the direction of participatory politics, the citizen as key participator in creating political life—such as the Greek *politēs* was—may disappear completely to be replaced by apathetic, mindless "nonelites" who at best vote occasionally and "orient" themselves periodically to increasingly distant and irresponsible oligarchs. At worst—and the worst seems confirmed by mounting empirical evidence—these so-called citizens will submerge themselves into a boundless lassitude of private fancies, leaving the political world above them to unchecked "activists," "elites," and "influentials."

What are these generalizations about citizenship?

First, the contours of basic political membership in all states limit the political space of those societies. This space is shaped by a dualist structure of tangible objects and subjective perceptions which arranges a system of shared political meanings among citizens and also establishes these meanings in hierarchies of valued priorities.[3] Around a nation are drawn a number of physical and nonphysical boundaries within which citizens feel at home, outside of which they are foreigners. Such a space is molded by objective factors such as geographical frontiers, an economic system, a legal system, a common political language or perhaps multiple, official languages (Canada, India, Switzerland), and by special governmental institutions called offices. But one also discovers certain subjective perceptions and expectations that members share about correct political action, expectations drawn from the members' own individual needs and values and from the social symbolism attributed to boundaries, economies, languages, and governments. These symbolic perceptions may not find common agreement throughout a nation. Nevertheless, there are often common relationships between more specialized perceptions which entitle an observer to speak of a "pattern" for even the heterogeneous political life of a Switzerland or an India, although not of a single "national character" (a difficult notion to apply to any country). In every political situation, no matter how transient, one can locate such patterns of civic expectations. The total space of subjective expectations, united with objective factors, represents the "political culture" of a national state.[4]

Second, the political culture, as the prevailing shape of political space, aims the citizen's attention *toward* certain political features and *away* from others. Some of the means employed for directing attention involve socialization processes whereby individuals and groups are drawn into the dominant ideology, or into one of the dominant ideologies, of a political culture. A wider education—varying with the society—also exists and prepares citizens for making independent and frequently idiosyncratic political judgments. Sometimes, liberalizing features are assiduously cultivated, opening the individual's mind to influences well beyond his immediate social background, but more often these broader influences are neglected or deliberately suppressed. Also mitigating the discipline of political socialization—the group mediation of political truth—are factors endemic to personality development, namely, biological and psychological traits which make for certain obvious and more subtle individual differences. Through this total preparation for making political judgments, a mixture of values (judgments of what ought to be) and beliefs (judgments about reality) are communicated to individuals and groups learning the ways of their political culture. Seldom, if ever, are these values and beliefs distinguished from each other, for political culture expects not only acceptance of its views on political reality but affirmation as well, not only objective verification but loyalty.

The cultural directions may often seem ambiguous and complicated, particularly as historical events intervene to generate crisis and change. Nevertheless, in spite of complexities, citizens do learn, by rote and subtle precept, *to expect* certain values and facts about politics to be truer than others, and *to neglect* areas of valuation and experience incongruent with their expectations (the latter process being a kind of immunization against *total* political reality). Authority, law, legitimacy, order, and power—all prominent features of government—become associated with special political patterns, not with politics in general. Hence, a frame of reference for assessing politics will be constructed from materials the citizen has scavenged among the artifacts of his culture. A liberal political education may aim, with varying dedication and success, to look at politics more generally, but "the political," as a generic concept, makes less sense to most persons than "American politics," "Soviet politics," and so on.

As a third generalization about citizenship, two "ideal-type" political cultures may be envisaged: One that gives citizens primary responsibility for governing themselves directly—a "politics of participation"—and one that grants the most important governmental responsibilities for making authoritative decisions to a select few acting in behalf of, or in spite of, the citizen body—a "politics of power." This distinction forms the foundation for the present essay.

Throughout history, citizens have known much more about power than participation. Some may even find it difficult to conceive of any alternative to power. The politics of power divides into two kinds of leadership: those who act "in behalf of"—a "politics of representation"—and those who act "in spite of"—a "politics of oligarchy." In either case, however, the few govern and the many are governed, a situation which is the most salient feature in any form of power politics. From this basic factor in power flow many consequences important for contemporary politics, not the least being a special political vocabulary. Plainly, power is identified here with hierarchy—those on top or nearer the top making more important decisions affecting the welfare of all group members, and thus having "more power" than those lower in the hierarchy. Power means the relatively greater ability some persons have to control (or dominate) a hierarchically structured group's resources. The more such ability one has, the more likely one will find oneself in the labyrinths of power with other powerful persons. Those in these labyrinths will be called "the powerful," a group which may not be knit together in a conspiracy against the less powerful, but a group drawn together, nevertheless, by a common expertise, their extraordinary aptitude—for a variety of reasons—to commandeer power.

This essay will contrast the two ideal types, participation and power, then narrow the issue to one between participation and representation, at this later point arguing that representation is now fading into more oligarchic forms of power. Both the politics of participation and the politics of power have distinctive political cultures involving objective political structures and subjective citizen expectations. The following chapters will draw contrasts between participation and power more completely.

Following from the dichotomy between power and participation is a fourth generalization about citizenship: Few political societies are totally controlled by either the politics of participation or the politics of power. Certain unorthodox, underdeveloped political practices and ideologies usually persist. Participatory politics, for example, does not vanish under the governance of power, but the latter will adapt participation's heresy to current realities, and if it fails to do this, may force "radical" and "revolutionary" areas of participatory power underground. (These radical areas are to be distinguished, of course, from forms of power that a given culture of power cannot abide, such as American culture's discrimination against the Communist Party. In the latter case both American government and Communism are forms of the politics of power.) Often, an orthodoxy so pervades a political culture under power politics that participants in unorthodox behavior see themselves, too, as radicals and revolutionaries. After a so-called revolution has won the day, some persons seem surprised that the political system has not changed as much as they had hoped or feared, because the revolutionaries have no conception of how to behave in positions of power other than the precepts taught them by those they have replaced.

Related to the four preceding characteristics of citizenship is a fifth. The prevailing image of political action in the West, at least since the late Middle Ages, has been one variant of the politics of power—representative government. Ostensibly, representation joins power with participation within an institutionalized setting and so achieves, the orthodox argue, a victory of participation over power *within limits* as the citizen body comes to control the power holders. Actually, in every form of representative politics the most typical feature is *plena potestas*, the arming

of select individuals, political parties, or other groups—more often professional agents than not—with plenary power to act in place of and with
the full authorization of the constituents, the ordinary citizens. There are
several versions of *plena potestas*, varying with the extent of such
authorization and ranging from constitutional democracy to modern totalitarianism (and this range of authorization is significant, of course).
Nevertheless, the plenary theme runs throughout. The representative is
placed in a special, superior position where he *and others like him*—
fellow representatives, together with their intimate associates—form
special groups charged with making state decisions, while constituents
arrange themselves into positions of partisanship. In all likelihood, fellow
representatives as well as subordinated henchmen develop an *esprit de
corps* within their respective groups. As fellow colleagues and experts in
organizing power, they steel themselves in a solidarity isolated, to greater
or lesser extent, from the citizen body. Major political decisions are then-
ceforth effectively protected from citizen activity, and the representatives
are further strengthened in their isolation by professional and secrecy
factors. Subsequent "orientation" of citizens to these leadership groups
comprises mainly a listless watching from the sidelines while a select few
actually act and create a politics. Under representative government the
politics of participation metamorphoses into a variety of spectator politics with audiences and players; the imagery of a "watchful citizenry"
applies here. As society grows more complicated, the typical pattern for
modern development, representation seems to be the only governmental
solution. But such complexity only isolates representatives still more
from their constituents and finally destroys representation altogether,
leading to more oligarchic varieties of power. Representation, as a form
of democracy where ordinary citizens govern themselves, at least nomi-
nally, becomes increasingly a hollow rationalization for rigidly hierarchical structures.[5]

The severity of hierarchical restrictions on action varies, but
everywhere spontaneity yields to official channels and procedures developed in the complexities of power. In this process the citizen becomes
alienated, or estranged, from authoritative political decisions created in
elaborate governmental structures, an alienation leading to powerlessness
and then to political incapacity. The ideology and practice of representation are so pervasive today that even in nonpublic areas of participation, such as private interest groups, or in areas such as universities (no
larger and often smaller than the largest of ancient Greek cities), representative institutions flourish as the normal means of governance; few
would think there was any practical *political* alternative. Thus the citizen
becomes steadily more restricted in his options for participation,

wherever he turns for political experience. As a consequence, civic virtue declines. When the ordinary citizen no longer participates, the ideologists appear who argue that most people care little about politics anyway and would just as soon immerse themselves completely in private matters such as making a livelihood and raising a family. Such indifference to public matters is taken as natural, the fault of human nature rather than of representative politics (a fallacious reasoning to be discussed fully in Chapter 3). Meanwhile, representatives in groups large and small, public and private, continue to wield plenary power and further reinforce this power, with assistance from competent auxiliary bureaucracies. Like the ancient praetorian auxiliaries, however, these bureaucracies increase their role to the point where their former masters now become their servants. Accompanying this ascendancy is a new argument which claims that bureaucracy is *more* representative than traditional institutions.[6]

The political culture of representation, as all cultures of power, develops an ideology (statements of fact masking values) that glamorizes the leaders, denigrates the led. This ideology of power is a sixth general characteristic of contemporary citizenship. Political drama concentrates on presidents, legislators, jurists, and generals. But who remains interested in the ordinary citizen? Does he even remain interested in himself? At most there is the political scientist concerned about the "responses" of the citizen audience to the drama of power politics; most current survey research is carried on in the spirit of the audience-actor relationship. Generations of youth and adults are socialized to think in terms of representative government as the only possible and practical form for their societies. So basic is the orthodoxy of representation that it sometimes becomes the one governmental principle firmly anchored in an otherwise boiling sea of political change, as in the "republican form" guaranteed every American state under the national constitution, and in the hoary fiction of "parliamentary supremacy" so deeply implanted in the English constitution. Furthermore, young people learn quite early that certain representative offices provide keys to the entire political structure, and this early awareness probably tends to support later habits of obedience and veneration. True, some versions of the doctrine of representation have specified that ultimately "the people shall judge" (John Locke) or have "the last say" (populistic democracy, according to Robert A. Dahl), but even these arguments place primary emphasis on leadership positions.[7] The idea of a final say held by the voting public applies only to individual candidates anyway, and not to their offices or to the structure of power. Called by the political scientist Karl Loewenstein "man's greatest political invention," representation becomes a utilitarian and moral virtue prized in the subjective imagination, while direct participation in defiance of the representative tradition can easily slip into the informal (at best) or subversive (at worst) category. As a result, man's "second greatest" political invention turns out to be the modern electoral party (Loewenstein), since it connects expanding popular participation in government to political leadership.[8] Representation presumably domesticates leadership in the name of participation, or at least it does so in its democratic varieties; actually, representation always starts from the assumption that power—some ruling, and most following—forms a necessary part of life. As a consequence of this assumption, representation domesticates participation for the sake of the politics of power by clouding the citizen's political vision with narcotic delights of popular control. Much truth is contained in the cynical jibe, "The King is dead, long live the King." This last truth seems especially verified when representative institutions decline in their importance, preparing the way not for expanded participation, but for more stringent oligarchies.

Related to this sixth general aspect of citizenship is a corollary: An important task confronting representative statesmen is to induce nonrepresentative participating areas, spaces where citizens directly create their own policies on certain issues and events in the spirit of spontaneous cooperation, to follow correct procedures and to form alliances with orthodox representative institutions. Barring this consummation, groups that remain outside the representative process, in particular those groups espousing an ideal of participation and opposing an ideal of power, are deprecated, persecuted, and even destroyed. What better spokesman could be found for this point of view than Thomas Hobbes, a leading theorist of representation, who distinguished in his *Leviathan* between officially authorized participatory groups and "unjust" factions of state, "as patricians, and plebeians of old time in Rome, and of aristocraticals and democraticals of old time in Greece"? The latter groups proved guilty, in Hobbes's judgment, of "being contrary to the peace and safety of the people, and. . .taking of the sword out of the hand of the sovereign." Though Hobbes also deprecated "factions for government of religion, as of Papists, Protestants, and so on," he conveniently found at hand a quotation from the New Testament, Acts 19:38–40, to footnote his argument.[9] Hobbes's virtue of honesty was also his vice, and he was accused of absolutism. But the archetypal liberal, John Stuart Mill, another theorist of representative government, drew a milder but similar distinction between official and unofficial (for Hobbes, lawful and unlawful). Mill advocated in his *Representative Government* that England convert its cumbersome nineteenth-century Parliament into a debating society representing diverse popular interests, at the same time, changing its electoral system into a sieve designed to segment public opinion into proportionate measures within the parliament. These recommendations aimed to accommodate participation within representation. Writing amid a crisis in the politics of representation, associated with a wider series of shocks within power politics over effectively governing more complex, democratized societies, Mill intended to save representation and preserve its ideology in the face of expanding areas of popular participation. For Mill the trouble called for better representation, not increased participation. (His friend, Alexis de Tocqueville, living in Bonapartist France during the mid-nineteenth century, worried more correctly about expanding oligarchic power in the name of popular democracy—Caesaristic democracy—at the expense of both energetic representative government and vital popular participation.[10])

Yet the citizen's main task is not to represent others as an agent in a governmental hierarchy but to be himself and to participate directly and spontaneously in creating public business. As he participates, he may come to represent, as a symbol might stand for more complicated reality, a government flowing from the joint efforts of its members. Authority, power, and success will be less important in these participative situations than the experience of participating together in a unique creation.

Contrasted to this common enterprise is the situation found today in which representatives form the government, citizens the governed. Political participation in its fullest sense is any spontaneous activity, open to all members, related to developing the common business of organizing a group (in this essay, the business of developing a *state*). What role does participation of this fullest sort play within a representative politics based on distinctions between the powerful and the many followers? This will be a major question with which to reckon. To answer this question, it will be necessary to contrast even more extensively in later chapters the politics of participation with the politics of representation, thus making clear what a small role participation plays in contemporary politics.

THE APPROACH OF THIS BOOK

As its over-all strategy, this essay will proceed from preliminary classification to examine how objective and subjective political cultures limit the expectations of citizens; in brief, how civic imagination achieves a type of spatial contour, a symbolic frame of reference linked to political actors, actions, settings, and interests. Then some consequences for contemporary citizenship which derive from the present political culture (the politics of representation) will be examined. Finally, it will be argued that the present contours of representative politics do not meet adequately the needs of those modern and modernizing societies which encourage complicated expectations from individuals and groups, but provide the societies with medieval means for achieving their ends. Either traditional representative institutions have proved unworkable in these dynamic settings, or they have operated only fretfully and inadequately. The first reaction of nations plagued by poor representative government is to adopt more extreme oligarchic solutions, as in those party-elite totalitarian regimes shaped by Nazi and Communist revolutions or in the various military governments that have gained ascendancy in large parts of Africa, Asia, the Middle East, and Latin America. Stronger leadership is always the panacea within the politics of power. Or in nations with long representative traditions, where ancient political institutions are buttressed by ironclad laws, convenient fictions, and patriotic sentiments, newer forces led by interest-group oligarchies and institutional bureaucracies have operated silently behind Old English and Early American façades. Although there may be exceptions, it seems evident that obsolete representative forms are challenged by even more restrictive forms of oligarchy, which deny even more completely the participative function of citizenship. But do the more novel forms of power succeed in meeting contemporary problems such as exploding populations, the havoc of war, worldwide racial tensions, inadequate diets, and the contradictory blessings of affluent societies? Have not these new oligarchies only made matters worse? After the failure of older forms of power politics, who has thought of turning away from accentuated power to a political system based more and more on participation? Perhaps the solution for questions as personal and spontaneous as population control, world peace, racial harmony, physical survival, and the cultural potentials of affluence, could best come from governments also personal and spontaneous—from a politics of participation. This prospect presents an enticing possibility for further exploration.

Notes to Chapter 1

1. *Trop v. Dulles*, 356 U.S. 100–102 (1958); *Perez V. Brownell*, 356 U.S. 64 (1958).
2. See the references made by Hannah Arendt to citizenship as official identity in *The Origins of Totalitarianism* 2d ed. (New York: Meridian Books, Inc., 1958) p. 287.

3. On the idea of "political space," see Sheldon S. Wolin, *Politics and Vision* (Boston: Little, Brown & Company 1960), p. 7.

4. A more detailed examination of "political culture" and "political socialization" is given in chapters 2 and 3 of this book.

5. Rousseau's fear of representative government can be found in *The Social Contract* (1762), Book 3, chapter 15.

6. The view that bureaucracy is more representative than traditional representative institutions can be found in Norton E. Long's essay, "Bureaucracy and Constitutionalism," in Charles Press, ed., *The Polity* (Chicago: Rand McNally & Company, 1962), Part 1, chapter 5.

7. On the theory of popular "last say" in modern democracy, see Robert A. Dahl, *A Preface to Democratic Theory* (Chicago: University of Chicago Press, 1956), pp. 36–51, 90–123.

8. On representative government, see Karl Loewenstein, *Political Power and the Governmental Process,* 2d ed. (Chicago: University of Chicago Press, 1956), p. 40; on political parties, Loewenstein, pp. 76–77. Loewenstein argues that "Politics is nothing else but the struggle for power" (p. 3). On politics as power and political science as the study of power, see Harold D. Lasswell and Abraham Kaplan, *Power and Society* (New Haven, Conn.: Yale University Press, 1950), Part 2, chapter 5. An emendation to this view is found in James March, "The Power of Power," in David Easton, ed., *Varieties of Political Theory* (Englewood Cliffs, N.J.: Prentice-Hall, Inc. 1966), chapter 3. For the view that if politics is power, citizenship becomes a question in power too, see Lasswell and Kaplan: "*Citizens* are those in a body politic who share in the allocation of power; *subjects,* those who do not" (p. 217).

9. Thomas Hobbes, *Leviathan* (1651), ed. by Michael Oakeshott (Oxford: Basil Blackwell & Mott, Ltd., 1955), Part 2, chapter 22, p. 15.

10. The exchanges between John Stuart Mill and de Tocqueville on mass society are interesting here. See Alexis de Tocqueville, *Correspondance Anglaise,* in *Oeuvres Complètes,* 12 vols., ed. by J. P. Mayer (Paris: Gallimard, 1954), Vol. VI, Part 2.

Chapter 2

A POLITICAL SYSTEM IS ANY PERSISTENT
PATTERN OF HUMAN RELATIONSHIPS THAT
INVOLVES TO A SIGNIFICANT EXTENT,
POWER, RULE, OR AUTHORITY. . . . ANY
COLLECTION OF REAL OBJECTS THAT IN-
TERACT IN SOME WAY WITH ONE ANOTHER
CAN BE CONSIDERED A SYSTEM. . . .

Robert A. Dahl
Modern Political Analysis

WELL, THEN, A COMMONWEALTH IS THE
PROPERTY OF A PEOPLE, BUT A PEOPLE IS
NOT ANY COLLECTION OF HUMAN BEINGS
BROUGHT TOGETHER IN ANY SORT OF WAY,
BUT AN ASSEMBLAGE OF PEOPLE IN LARGE
NUMBERS ASSOCIATED IN AGREEMENT WITH
RESPECT TO JUSTICE AND A PARTNERSHIP
FOR THE COMMON GOOD. . . . FOR WHAT IS
A STATE EXCEPT AN ASSOCIATION OR PART-
NERSHIP IN JUSTICE. . . .?

Cicero
De Re Publica

2

Objective Political Culture

This essay's main concerns are, first, to draw contrasts between two kinds of politics—the politics of participation and the politics of power—in such a way that light can be shed on problems in contemporary citizenship and, second, to deal with how and why the "political cultures" of these two types of politics differ. The constructing of ideal types may have a mentally stimulating effect in itself, but as Weber pointed out, their chief function is to order experience. Hence, such concepts as power and participation, when used as ideal types, ought eventually to touch upon the vagaries of real cultures in order to show, in practical terms, how ideas and actions might differ in the two politics. As the elder Mill once reminded his young son, the question is not theory *and* practice, but good theory conforming to experience and bad theory which does not. Chapter 1 introduced a classification of ideal types, and it is now time to relate these ideal types to the artifacts and attitudes that are associated with genuine political life.

If, as one anthropologist has put it, "Culture is the man-made part of the environment," then political culture represents that area of human artifice devoted to organizing people in common undertakings to meet and to resolve social differences with minimization of violence.[1] The definition of politics can wait for later expansion. At this point, as preparation for the argument in this and the next chapter, it is only necessary to stay close to the notion that politics is part of culture, and that a culture exhibits (*a*) tangible representations, in the form of objects or artifacts, including histories, literatures, languages, and the like; and (*b*) intangible subjective dimensions related to human beings. In other words, every political culture consists of political objects and subjective perceptions concerning those objects. This chapter will concentrate on the objective side of political culture, the actors, events, and settings that provide focus for civic enterprises, while the next chapter will discuss the lines of transmission between objects and individuals in subjective political culture. Objective political culture *demands* attention from the citizenry; subjective political culture *directs* the attention of the citizenry.

Viewing politics first as a system of political objects and then as a structure of subjective perceptions provides an analytical convenience and nothing more, as with the delimitations in Chapter 1, since the ways in which attention and imagination are stimulated by political objects depend in large measure on subjective factors governing attention and imagination. Nevertheless, given the above caveat that political events and perceptions inextricably weave together in experience, one can still speak profitably, if guardedly, about political objects.

Imagine a continuous stage, a panorama where certain objects tend to attract attention and limit imagination. As common sights and sounds of a political culture, these objects become familiar to the point of being self-evident. Familiarity, in turn, prompts feelings of security. When unfamiliar political objects are introduced, the tendency on the part of citizens is to retreat toward more solid ground, even to the point of developing rationalizations (excuses) that *only* the familiar is practical for their political culture. In the politics of power, for example, citizens find elaborate hierarchy both familiar and practical, while spontaneous participation seems strange and unworkable.

All cultures are distinguished by those artifacts they lavish with attention and those they neglect.[2] Political cultures are no different. Usually, power's obvious characteristics dominate the public's imagination. Displaying little prominence, on the other hand, is participation; its distinctive political culture appears strange. Participation may be defeated within a power culture not only for reasons of governmental repression and civic education, but because it is subdued from the outset through poor public exposure (either because participation looks "bad" or because it cannot be seen at all). A poor exposure deeply rooted in cultural tradition encourages repression and neglect, and these in turn discourage publicity. Yet participation's weaknesses within the contemporary politics of power would not extend to situations where participation achieves prominence and power declines in importance: As one moves from power to a more participative form of politics, objective and subjective political cultures change their distinctive emphases.

What are the political objects which so fix attention that they literally *demand* this attention? How do they operate, and why do they work as they do? One may classify political objects under four headings: (1) actors, (2) actions, (3) settings, and (4) interests.[3]

POLITICAL ACTORS

Among those most prominent in any society are actors engaged in deciding questions in governmental situations where controversy and the need for conciliation arise. These persons are political actors. There are official and unofficial actors of this type, but public attention usually fixes on occupants of prominent offices, while it is diverted from other offices and from unofficial sectors. Such focusing results from long acculturation. So accustomed are people to turning their attention to powerful figures, that they even call entire historical periods after some gaudy personage, as in "The Napoleonic Era," "The Age of Jackson," and so on, despite the fact that millions of actors—other leaders and ordinary citizens—played parts.[4]

Government comprises the structure of official positions for a society. Official positions never appear in isolation; they are ranked by the order in which government places them. Objectively speaking, modern states rank certain officers in high positions and then range downward to the lowliest, ordinary offices. In most cases, the higher positions coincide with those who are more powerful in government, the officials and the unofficial groups identified with a particular position, while at lower positions ordinary citizens perform their duties. At the lowest ranks of governmental duty one hardly thinks of the tasks performed as public ones at all—though they may be—so identified is politics with power in modern political cultures. Rather, one speaks of a "private citizen" (the lowest civilian rank) and a "private soldier" (the lowest military rank).

More often than not, where the politics of power monopolizes attention, people no longer think of the citizen as a public officeholder at all, though citizenship is an official status and the citizen is an officeholder.[5] The citizenship position retains all the legal status of any other office in the state, though citizens do not usually wear identifying uniforms or insignia and seldom occupy office buildings specially assigned to them. In fact, uniforms, insignia, and special facilities are symbols that dramatize positions in order to put such statuses in the public eye.

(There are sometimes official symbols that stigmatize too.) When reminded of the truism that a citizen is a lawful public official, most persons would agree with the logic but probably add that a citizen is not nearly as important an official as an American President or even a tax collector. These same persons would probably pay homage to the great value of individual citizens for the American system of government but at the same time think citizenship an unimportant official status within that system. Leaders are noticed because they are given prominence, whereas citizens are ignored because nothing distinguishes them as officials. Political cultures such as the United States, ostensibly built on the doctrine of popular sovereignty, spend the vast bulk of their resources insuring the continued prominence of a few.

Political actors include all public officers, but it is more precise to say that "actors" are those seen by an audience. Such actors figure prominently on a public stage. Although one can speak in general of political actors, whether they occupy prominent positions in political life or not, real actors live in prominence. In actual politics every society is characterized by the actors to whom it gives important positions on the public stage, just as that society is distinguished by the kinds of emphases it gives to various cultural subjects. The prevailing political culture determines who will stand out as a political actor, but today those who become outstanding represent most often the politics of power, not participation. Trained by experience and by rote to distinguish between elites and nonelites, leaders and led, powerful and powerless, it is not surprising that the public supports this world of political experience and no other. Experience excites certain expectations, which in turn trigger perceptions. In a closed circle of reinforcement, perceptions echo back messages from both experience and expectation (see the discussion of "feedback" in Chapter 3).

The actor-audience relationship becomes all-pervasive as it affects the vocabulary of politics. Citizens sit in the dark, encouraging with their occasional applause the prominent players. In turn, the actors play "roles," or perhaps the audience too has its "role," as it is written into the play for occasional small parts. Citizens learn to view political action as drama or game; in either case, the notion of featured actors or players seems appropriate, as do the ideas of role and audience. Given the sometimes elaborate codes of conduct binding players together, it may take patience for members of the audience to discover rules for the game, plus those special languages and motivation that encourage *esprit de corps* among the actors. Much political science research deals with deciphering these rules, languages, and motivations.

Even if these rules can be discovered by the outsider in an audience, it does not make that outsider a full-fledged player. Simple knowledge gives him no power. He must wait for admission or insinuate his way into the charmed circle legally or illegally.[6] Rousseau's fears about representative institutions are everywhere confirmed within the politics of power: Leaders, players or actors become isolated by the nature of their joint efforts from an audience which usually can only appreciate, but seldom join in, the collaboration.[7] Some types of democratic political theory invite the audience—the large mass of ordinary citizens—to participate occasionally in certain aspects of leadership, as in periodic elections, but this is something like asking a person without expertise, but with information gained from watching television on Sunday afternoons, to play for one day on a professional football team. The occasional player gathers little experience, never gains the team's confidence, contributes nothing to the joint enterprise, and because of his inexperience runs the risk of serious injury. Regrettably, modern citizens resemble these occasional players.[8]

As citizens are called upon to do less in the dynamics of power politics, they begin to become marginal to the area of really important political decisions, and, in turn, attention is averted from them. Decisionmakers increasingly think more of each other's reactions. Being less important than other officials, citizens lose their interest in politics as something relevant to their lives. As relatively insignificant actors, what can ordinary citizens accomplish? Why not turn to more private areas of interest where the individual still counts for something?

It seems a promising hypothesis that the citizen's role, as a political participant with genuine responsibilities for the common social order, is as much minimized by the dynamics of modern political cultures—or perhaps by political cultures in nearly every historical period—as this role is curtailed by any natural aversion of ordinary people to involve themselves politically. Politics, the most artificial of social enterprises, is part of man-made culture: *Local political culture, not universal human nature,* presents the great barrier to wider civic participation. Enough conventional wisdom has been expended in contemporary political science about how most people busy themselves with nonpublic concerns relating to family, job, and recreation. But most people have no choice, because to become "engaged" politically will no doubt only lead to frustration concerning the really important political decisions. Many vote for special officials, but only these officials make life-and-death decisions affecting many. If many persons (tens of millions) are to be incinerated in thermonuclear war, *should* only a few make the decision to begin this incineration? Or is the argument that whatever should be the case, the few *will* make this decision? If it is the latter, there is no choice for most persons about so fundamental a question, and there is no reason why they should not feel frustrated, inefficacious, apathetic, or perhaps blindly outraged. This hypothesis can be expressed as a simple syllogism:

> Governing involves choosing and making decisions.
> Most people have no choice in the most important political matters.
> *Therefore*, most persons will not engage in governing either affairs of state or their own destinies in so far as their destinies are politically determined.

The best defense against frustration is not to become frustrated in the first place. Apathy is one good defense.

POLITICAL ACTION

Political events result from the actions of political actors. Again, as with the actors themselves, every political culture concentrates on some events and neglects others. In the politics of power the most important actions are those generated by the powerful.

Action flows from decision. One of the basic approaches to the study of political action concentrates on decision making, with primary attention devoted to the powerful. Even with an accent on decisions made by ordinary citizens, as in the many voting studies conducted by American political scientists, the main concern is with how voters orient themselves toward the powerful as candidates for public office, as makers of issues, and as leaders of parties and other interest groups. The main emphasis in the decision-making approach invariably centers on great leaders and their underlings.[9] The question of what the act of voting signifies for the citizen's *own* personal development, as contrasted with what this act means for the development of leaders, is seldom if ever asked. Even when voting studies introduce the idea of "alienation," a highly personal question about individual and group estrangement from the prevailing political culture, the interest seems to lie much more in how alienation relates to the task of leadership than in what alienation means for the task of citizenship.[10]

Once decisions are made, actions follow. Frequently, such actions seem very complicated and actors appear trapped in webs of irony. Historians and other students of the past concern themselves today principally with the powerful—particularly with successful leaders—and the twists of history relating to the politics of power. Much attention is lavished on kings, generals, prime ministers, revolutionary figures, and presidents. But scarcely a word is devoted to the involvements of citizens, as citizens, in the course of historical events. In fact, no one has yet written a history of the development of citizenship from ancient Greece to the present.[11]

To act politically means to participate in political events. Every person having an official status in politics participates simply by adopting some point of view relative to politics. This kind of activity constitutes a symbolic participation.[12] Various political cultures assign different weights to the points of view found among their citizenry. The politics of power always gives great credence to the values, beliefs, and attitudes of those who are leaders, while less importance is assigned to opinions lower in the official structure. Events are largely determined within this form of politics by the wishes of those who lead, simply because those at the top may always choose to ignore the viewpoints of ordinary citizens. On the other hand, ordinary citizens can hardly avoid the consequences of public acts performed by those above them in government. Not infrequently, even in the most animated of representative democracies, citizens are confronted with *faits accomplis* by their leaders.

Participation also means overt action as well as symbolic action. Here again cultures attribute different values to different forms of open participation. Some forms of action are so highly esteemed that special terms are attached to them which distinguish these forms, and the events stirred by such actions, from more mundane activities. Thus the political participation of leaders in the politics of power is no longer called by the term "participation" at all, but becomes "representation" or "adjudication" or "administration." Meanwhile, the ordinary citizen "participates," a less honorific form of action. This is what was meant earlier by the idea that the citizen's primary function is to participate, and in this sense all citizens are free and equal, whether they participate as leaders or followers. But the politics of power makes hierarchical distinctions which in effect divide common participation by all citizens into special forms of action pursued by leaders, and general forms undertaken by ordinary persons. This politics then concentrates its rewards on the special kinds of action associated with leadership rather than on common participation. With such distinctions basic to political order, it becomes difficult to speak of a "common interest" or "common involvement" among "fellow citizens." Participatory politics is egalitarian; power politics is not. In the first case, citizens look *horizontally* to friends, associates, equals; in the second case, they look *vertically* to their government. The power state is inimical to commonwealth, if by commonwealth one means, as this essay does, a community sharing in certain vital responsibilities and privileges.

Citizen action as envisaged by representative democracy deserves special attention, because, as one form of the politics of power, such democracy seemingly disproves the contention made here that power politics invariably denigrates citizen participation. Supposedly, in representative situations where there is "government by the people," popular participation is given high status and expansive latitude. Indeed, representative democracies promote the popular myth of a rational, omnicompetent citizen, jealously guarding his freedom against powerful predators—a myth no responsible democratic theorist ever believed (see Chapter 3). Most often, the criticism levelled against this exalted notion of government by the people centers on two things, the myth of the rational citizen (the myth proves chimerical) and the quantity of actual participation (the quantity proves disappointingly low). Our criticism here will be somewhat different: While adhering to the ideal of citizen participation, representative democracy (an improvement over some other forms of power politics) consistently encourages low-quality citizen action by making a fetish out of only one form of political participation—voting. Chapters 3 and 4 will deal with representation and voting in greater detail, as these activities relate to contemporary citizenship.

POLITICAL SETTINGS

Important elements in objective political culture are the settings or scenes for actors and actions. These scenes include *geographical boundaries, political languages,* and *economic systems.* All three kinds of settings contribute to the prevailing shape of political space, whether this space is a variant of the politics of power or of the politics of participation.

It would be difficult to imagine modern politics without the national state, and impossible to conceive of this state without physical, territorial frontiers. Surrounding these boundaries are a whole group of political objects pertaining to these boundaries, all tending to reinforce the politics of power. Foremost among these objects are the representatives of national sovereignty in both domestic and international affairs. On the international level actors and actions frankly aim for protection of national power interests, that is, for maintenance or advancement of a nation's position within the hierarchy of world "powers." Here the struggle for power is more naked than one usually finds in domestic politics. Foreign affairs require an expertise quite outside the competence of ordinary citizens, which in turn gives representatives even more leeway in international matters than at home. Furthermore, this expertise enhances the status of leaders within their own states. For the sake of national defense and power aggrandizement in the name of the nation, hierarchical power seems particularly justified. More than elsewhere in politics, the great bulk of the world's citizens stand by as a mute audience watching the spectacle of competing international hierarchies, largely uncontrolled except by each other's power strategies.

Participatory politics seems especially out of place in the context of international relations, although when one turns from conflict to cooperation for peace, the picture changes somewhat and the beneficial potentials of participation by private citizens appear much greater. An example of this participation is found in the so-called "Pugwash Conferences," originated in 1957, which are held among scientists from East and West on matters of world policy that relate to scientific discovery and technology. Although there is bound to be some suspicion parallelling international controversies, even among scientists, the conferences have proved remarkable for their dispassionate discussion of vital problems such as thermonuclear war. There is little official sponsorship of scientists who attend, save from national scientific agencies in the cases of Communist participants (who could only attend this way, since there are no "private" foundations in Communist countries). In fact, the idea is to de-emphasize official connections in the hope that something may be accomplished outside the competition for power. A general feeling persists among those who have attended Pugwash meetings, that given the prestige of science and the important role that scientists play in all modern states, these conferences have done much to ease international tensions over scientific matters, especially in the field of nuclear warfare.

As languages essential to carrying on the common business of organizing societies, the vocabularies of politics may also be treated as objects. Since these languages are symbolic, they obviously depend for their use on subjective factors. But political words—legal language, for instance—do provide a tangible reserve from which cultures draw significance. The likelihood that expressions can be communicated to others in politics varies with the availability and status of certain languages. The problem of competing languages within a single political system, as when a large Communist Party exists in a capitalist country, is well known. At this juncture, however, the prime interest concerns how civic imagination seems automatically drawn toward certain aspects of politics and seems averted from others. In the politics of power, as noted in the previous section of this chapter, participation may itself be phrased in the vocabulary of power. Thus, voting becomes the most widespread form of civic participation in representative democracy, though in reality this form is oriented toward power, not individual participation. Voting's main objective is to develop winning candidates and party governments, not to produce strong citizens. A special vocabulary of participation, largely divorced from power, can be developed, as in the languages of Greek politics and in the theories of Rousseau, Proudhon, Gandhi, and others, but under most circumstances it is apt to appear utopian—out of place— when compared to the vocabulary of political power. Political languages are often expressed in the form of rules binding on actors; such rules may be formal laws or unwritten civic norms.

One of the chief objective factors in political cultures is the economic system. Statistics provide quantitative indexes for a national economy, and these indexes express a special setting for politics. The exact relationships between economics and politics have stimulated much debate, but some generalizations seem fairly plausible. Given the fact that much political conflict concerns economic matters (meaning by economic matters, the distribution of goods and services), it is reasonable to expect that political hierarchies would be sensitive to the demands of powerful groups within the economic structure. Hence, a political culture of unequal power might parallel an economic system with uneven distribution of wealth, at many points linking with this system in lateral, mutually beneficial alliances. This does not mean that the exact shape of political culture will resemble in every detail the economic structure within it, but that significant reciprocal relationships will exist between politics and economics. Furthermore, it seems a promising hypothesis that such relationships will perpetuate both a politics of power and an uneven economic distribution. Even where a national economy is ostensibly moving toward equal distribution, as in the Soviet Union, one can see this reinforcing relationship at work between power politics and economic structure. It is interesting that in the Soviet case political inequality, typified by the elitist position of the Communist Party, has fostered a "new class" with unequal economic advantages, or at least Milovan Djilas, a leading Yugoslav Communist, has argued this thesis in his book *The New Class*.[13] Since the Party is vested with exclusive power to own property in the name of the Soviet community, it combines in one agency disproportionate economic and political power. In noncommunist nations, politics and economics must form coalitions between the powerful in one sector and the powerful in the other. Significantly, the language of power comes more naturally to those higher on both the political and economic scales, while the vocabulary of participation is more likely to be used by those lower in *both* political and economic structures (until the latter finally become so frustrated that revolutionary power becomes a *cri du désespoir*, as in "proletarian power" and "black power").

Certain settings—geographical, linguistic, economic—contribute significantly, therefore, to the shape of political culture by occupying the center of the public stage. *Geographical frontiers* along the lines of national boundaries encourage dramatic conflict, though they are not entirely responsible for the frictions among nations. They also stimulate notions of national interest relative to other states. Accent thus falls on power, sovereignty, defense, and even territorial aggrandizement. A hierarchy of nations with greater and lesser power, each defending its sovereign interests, becomes the prevailing image of international politics for ordinary citizens. Such an image is more competitive than cooperative. *Political language* forms a reservoir of expressions, some used more frequently than others and hence some more readily accepted as normal or relevant for a society. The vocabulary of power is well-developed and constantly used, while the language of participation, though an integral part of the Western political tradition, is likely to be considered utopian. *Economic systems* cross over to political systems in alliances among hierarchies—with power, the more natural language, higher in the hierarchy and participation more likely lower down.[14]

POLITICAL INTERESTS

Closely related to actors, actions, and settings are political interests. Interests represent the goals actors wish to achieve through their actions within the objective settings of their political culture. Here, as with other objective aspects, interests are either more or less acceptable, depending upon the prevailing politics, power or participation. Which goals prove most prevalent depends upon the shape of political space, including the all-important subjective culture discussed in the next chapter, and in turn these goals help contour that space.

In the politics of power, political interests largely aim for improved positions within hierarchies. Because there are other interests directed toward the same goal, competition and conflict result. Goal orientation within the politics of power, therefore, centers on power and conflict among interests competing for ascendancy in the well-known "group struggle."[15] As with all other objective aspects of power politics, attention among participants centers on conflict for leadership positions and for the policies which emanate from such positions.

Blocs of interests, or "interest groups," prevail in the politics of power. These groups are then organized internally as hierarchical structures often more severe than those found in the national government itself. Such rigid organization proves necessary because these groups are in combat with other groups. Where a group is initially disadvantaged, as were workers' parties in Europe during the late nineteenth and early twentieth century, it may require an even more disciplined organization than its opponents. After power has been achieved, rigidity may lessen, though in nearly every interest group there appears a tendency to retain and strengthen oligarchy.[16]

Within these interest groups, conflict also develops for positions of power. Thus a form of politics arises inside individual groups as well as between groups. The result of this politics is more accent on power. Aspiring group leaders often take their ambitions for internal power into their group's relations with other groups, thus identifying their group's interests with their own. It is not uncommon to find interest groups whose goals reflect the personal idiosyncrasies of their leaders.

Compromise provides the best means for settling group conflicts. Since the struggle for power is theoretically without limits, some kind of control, short of duel to the death, has to be improvised. There are other ways for peacefully settling disputes about goals besides compromise, of course, provided that the disputes can proceed without any competition among interest groups for ascendancy. Two men arguing about whether money or poverty should be life's main goal might settle matters by some rational agreement to disagree, for this is a world of relative values. But neither man is competing for anything with the other, nor is he giving up anything valuable in the process of tolerating the other's position. To compromise under these circumstances would be to admit that the dispute is tantamount to competition and could end in worse consequences than each making a concession. Compromise is a socio-political convenience, not a philosophical principle; compromising proves necessary only in competitive situations where the alternative to not compromising is much worse. To compromise oneself is morally repugnant to many persons, for it involves giving away part of what one values, but the settling of competing political interests requires such a gift in the name of both interest-group success and social peace. Some have argued that the practice of compromise has something to do with toleration and relativist ethics, such as the two men agreeing to disagree. But perhaps this argument confuses what amounts to a necessity within the politics of power with philosophic principles that grant no concessions regarding one's own values. Toleration does not assume competition, but disagreement (two very different types of conflict).[17]

Certain interests in the politics of power may deviate from approved goals to more participatory ones. Simply because these goals are different from expected group aims, they may prove at least temporarily attractive to some persons within a political culture. In modern India, for example, a type of nonpower politics has developed, the *sarvodaya* movement, which aims, not at leadership, but at an impact on human personality.[18] The most notable goal of *sarvodaya* has been *bhoodan*, a campaign for land redistribution which appeals to the hearts of large land-owners for land gifts. This campaign has not been very successful, and events now indicate a steady evolution of the movement toward standard interest-group power politics. But it is an interesting example of both a role for participatory politics in a power-oriented society, and of the ten-uousness of such efforts in the face of more standard interest patterns. Significantly, since 1963 the *sarvodaya* has turned its efforts from *bhoodan* to *gramdan*, communal villages. In the latter area of com-munity development the Indian government is vitally interested, and the movement feels it can obtain greater advantages for the poor peasantry with a *gramdan* emphasis. This transition of *sarvodaya* seems to illus-trate, among other things, a perhaps inevitable tendency for participatory groups that desire success within the culture of power to change their goals in accordance with prevalent interest patterns in their culture; in this case, to align a group identified with nonpower politics with the more normal politics of regular government. Nevertheless, the *sarvodaya* movement represents a most significant experiment in the use of politics to instill feelings of human worth and personal development in land-owners and peasants. It is a true instance of allowing ordinary citizens to use politics for improving the quality of their humanity rather than as a means to gain ascendancy in a context of power, competition, and compromise. Gandhi's influence is evident.

The idea that politics has something to do with improving the quality of individual humanity will be pursued more thoroughly in the next chapters. This idea is as old as ancient Athens and as new as contem-porary India. It is found in both normative works in political theory and in empirical studies that relate spontaneous political activism to com-munity mindedness, tolerance for others, and personal maturation. The convergence of normative and empirical theory on the subject of partici-patory politics will receive special attention in Chapter 5.

Notes to Chapter 2

1. Melville Herskovits, *Man and His Works* (New York: Alfred A. Knopf, 1951), p. 17. On the idea of "economy of violence," with special reference to Machiavelli, see Sheldon S. Wolin, *Politics and Vision* (Boston: Little, Brown &

Company, 1960), pp. 220–224. Some might argue that politics may require a *maximization* of violence, but such a maximization could also signify a breakdown in political expertise.

2. On cultural "focus," see Herskovits, Part 6, chapter 32. The notion of political culture is developed somewhat differently in Gabriel Almond and Sidney Verba, *The Civic Culture* (Princeton, N.J.: Princeton University Press, 1963), Part 1, chapter 1; and differently again in Samuel H. Beer and Adam Ulam, eds., *Patterns of Government, The Major Political Systems of Europe*, 2d ed. (New York: Random House, Inc., 1962), pp. 32–45.

3. The division here into actors, actions, settings, and interests bears certain resemblances to Kenneth Burke's "five key terms of dramatism" in *A Grammar of Motives* (New York: Meridian Books, Inc., 1962), p. xvii. The parallels are intentional—the relative prominence of political objects varies a good deal with the dramatization of these objects. See also Murray Edelman, *The Symbolic Uses of Politics* (Urbana, Ill.: University of Illinois Press, 1964).

4. In this sense, Leo Tolstoy was a more prescient political analyst in his novel *War and Peace* than many a historian of the "Napoleonic Era."

5. On citizenship as an official position, see Joseph Tussman, *Obligation and the Body Politic* (New York: Oxford University Press, 1960), pp. 105ff.

6. On legal entrance into the charmed circles of power, see Vilfredo Pareto's theory of "the circulation of elites," in his *Mind and Society*, 4 vols., trans. by A. Bongiorno and A. Livingstone (New York: Harcourt, Brace & World, Inc., 1935), Vol. III, para. 2025–2058. Note also the idea of "access."

7. See Jean Jacques Rousseau, *The Social Contract* (1762), Book 3, chapter 15. See also Heinz Eulau, "Changing Views of Representation," in Ithiel de Sola Pool, ed., *Contemporary Political Science: toward Empirical Theory* (New York: McGraw-Hill Book Company, 1967), pp. 53–85, at p. 80.

8. The nature of the contemporary American political audience is summed up in Marshall McLuhan's idea of the "corporate participation" of the television audience in current events, *Understanding Media* (New York: McGraw-Hill, Inc., 1964), chapter 31. The fact that this audience is so "cool," even in the face of very exciting political happenings (such as the assassination of President John F. Kennedy), gives some idea of how domesticated participation is today, though McLuhan is sanguine.

9. The latest explanation of Michigan Survey Research Center voting studies reveals this elitist preoccupation. See Donald E. Stokes, "Dynamic Elements of Contests for the Presidency," *American Political Science Review*, LX (March 1966), 27. The earlier SRC study, *The American Voter*, abridged edition, by Angus Campbell and Others (New York: John Wiley & Sons, Inc., 1964), takes the politics of power as a "given" (p. 4).

10. See Murray B. Levin, *The Alienated Voter, Politics in Boston* (New York: Holt, Rinehart and Winston, Inc., 1960), p. 73, where the ideal of the powerful citizen in democratic theory is called "one of the sources of political alienation." In effect, feeling powerless flows from thinking too big!

11. At best, there are the following historical summaries: H. J. Haarhoff, *The Stranger at the Gate* (Boston: The Beacon Press, 1951); Werner Jaeger, *Paideia, The Ideals of Greek Culture*, 3 vols., trans. by Gilbert Highet (Oxford: Basil Blackwell & Mott, Ltd., 1954); Charles E. Merriam, *The Making of Citizens, A Comparative Study of Methods of Civic Training* (Chicago: University of Chicago Press, 1931); H. Mark Roelofs, *The Tension of Citizenship: Private*

Man and Public Duty (New York: Holt, Rinehart and Winston, Inc., 1957);
A. N. Sherwin-White, *The Roman Citizenship* (Oxford: Oxford University Press, 1939).

12. Edelman, chapter 9.

13. Milovan Djilas, *The New Class* (New York: Frederick A. Praeger, Inc., 1957), pp. 37–69.

14. The true meaning of the "power elite" argument of C. Wright Mills, as set forth in *The Power Elite* (New York: Oxford University Press, 1959). Such links are never automatic, in his estimation, they depend on social setting and skill.

15. First conceptualization of the "group struggle" can be found in Arthur F. Bentley, *The Process of Government* (1908), although to Madison and Marx go credit for earlier conceptions of this struggle in primarily economic terms, but each within a distinctive sociological perspective (for Madison, "faction"; for Marx, "class"; for Bentley, "group" and "interest"). Bentley admitted that he came into the study of politics from economics, and he hoped his study would teach him something about economics.

16. Although Robert Michels' "Iron Law of Oligarchy" has become somewhat unfashionable in political science, it still finds important backing in sociology. I would agree with the appreciation expressed for Michels in Philip Selznick's, *TVA and the Grass Roots* (New York: Harper and Row, Publishers, 1966), p. ix. Also, Selznick concludes his study with a recommendation that scope for participation must be found within modern administration, a prescription supported by the present essay as well.

17. The argument for casual relations between relativist ethics and toleration has best been presented by Hans Kelsen, "Foundations of Democracy," *Ethics*, LXVI (October 1955), 1–101. See also Hannah Arendt, "Politics and Truth," *The New Yorker*, XLIII (February 25, 1967), 49–88; and Tussman, chapter 4, on three misconceptions about democracy.

18. For a concise discussion of *sarvodaya*, see Gene D. Overstreet, " 'Non-power' Politics: The Sarvodaya Movement," in James B. Christoph, ed., *Cases in Comparative Politics* (Boston: Little, Brown & Company, 1965), pp. 472–498.

Chapter 3

MEN SEEK FOR VOCABULARIES THAT WILL
BE FAITHFUL *REFLECTIONS* OF REALITY. TO
THIS END, THEY MUST DEVELOP VOCABU-
LARIES THAT ARE *SELECTIONS* OF REALITY.
AND ANY SELECTION OF REALITY MUST, IN
CERTAIN CIRCUMSTANCES, FUNCTION AS A
DEFLECTION OF REALITY.

Kenneth Burke
A Grammar of Motives

3

Subjective Political Culture

By this time it should be clear that the familiar dichotomy
between "fact" (what is—empirical) and "value" (what ought to
be—normative) proves unsatisfactory here. By diverting and
averting attention, political objects control the imagination in arbitrary
ways. In effect, what is perceived as reality becomes, in the politics of
power, for instance, only what one is most used to—what attracts attention. Instead of seeing politics as a wide range of relationships, some
hierarchical and others participatory, whereby humans organize themselves in common undertakings to meet and to resolve their differences
with a minimization of violence, only the power side of these relationships is seen. Objective research then focuses only on power relationships
as empirical ones, despite the much broader potentialities (and actualities
from time to time) of politics. One of the great self-evident truths held by
many persons is that power constitutes the most important ingredient of
politics, and the quest for and acquisition of power constitute the most
·salient activity. They are right about the politics of power, but wrong
about politics more generally; in effect, they have become ideologists of
power. Political objects thus limit the vision of participants in politics.
But this limitation is immeasurably strengthened by subjective political
culture, the topic of this chapter.

Chapter 2 discussed political objects at length, and it is now time to examine the subjective aspects of political culture. Here the question concerns *how* citizens receive messages from the political actors, actions, settings, and interests surrounding them. Message is an expression used in communications theory to mean information in the form of cues that stimulate a receiver—in this case, a citizen—to act in certain ways. The actions of citizens, prompted by messages in the form of information cues about the objective political environment, become manifest in the form of activities taking place within political statuses. Every citizen occupies the citizenship status, but how he responds to this status constitutes his "citizenship role."[1] Styles will vary within limits established by the political culture. The way citizens play their role will affect, in turn, the politics of their culture, whether a politics primarily centered on participation or power.

With these initial considerations in mind, a four-phased paradigm for subjective political culture relevant to this analysis can be constructed. This paradigm proves necessary for organizing thought about political culture into objective and subjective components and for understanding the relationships between the workings of these components and the prevailing configuration of a culture, whether it is participation or power. First, are the political objects, including the citizenship status, comprising the environment in which citizens are expected to act. Second, there exist political communications links, or methods by which the environment communicates information to citizens about how political roles ought to be played. Third, the citizen responds to these messages by assuming the citizenship status and acting out his version of the role of the citizen. And fourth, the styles in which citizens perform their role as citizens will affect the prevailing politics of a culture, even while that politics controls to a considerable extent the options available for role playing; in communications terminology, there develops a "feedback" from citizen to political culture.

The present chapter deals with phases two, three, and four in this model, each a crucial element in the subjective side of political culture. How each stage functions will depend upon whether the prevailing political culture is one of participation or power, something readily ascertained by observing which political objects are emphasized as well as which kinds of communications and subjective responses prevail.

POLITICAL COMMUNICATIONS

Communications in general, and political communications in particular, have two aspects—the methods of communications and the contents of communications. Communications *methods* in political culture involve two different types, group-dominated "political socialization" and personal "political education." The *substance* of communications, as directed from culture to citizen, concerns the citizenship status and acceptable styles for playing roles within this status, in brief, standards for "good citizenship." The two methods of communications and the substance of political communications will receive attention in this section.

Political socialization, the first method of communication from culture to citizen, is that political truth which is mediated by groups to their members.[2] It is important to note that accent here centers on mediating or *giving* bases for values (judgments about good and bad, right and wrong, ought and ought not) and beliefs (popular knowledge of the political environment) to citizens. One might call these the "givens" of a political culture, or the "mores," as William Graham Sumner once entitled them.[3] Favorable reception by individuals of these mores emanating from groups (and there may be conflicting truths if one belongs to diverse groups) hinges on attitudes (predispositions to accept truths) that persons have about their environment. Political socialization pays much attention, therefore, to deliberately shaping attitudes instead of simply presenting values and beliefs cafeteria-style for the consideration of citizens. This means that socialization processes include psychological conditioning in the sense that Charles E. Merriam meant by his expression "the making of citizens."[4] Such deliberate manufacturing of civic responses include both manifest and latent efforts; that is, certain forms of socialization are readily apparent in the form of hortative books and so forth, while other forms of socialization involve relatively silent environmental conditioning.[5]

Manufacturing of consent or the making of citizens means that objective forces outside the manufactured product are working on that product. Clearly, in political socialization the really responsible agents are social ones, not individuals. As a result, the group, not the individual, has a "point of view" into which the member is inducted or initiated after proper conditioning. Nations, which are actually conglomerations of individuals, have their "interests." Political science prefers the language of "group interest" to that of individual self-interest. Although there is no need to adopt here any notion of a group mind, it is still possible to use the language of nineteenth- and twentieth-century sociology and political science, which is rich in expressions about how the group appears "other" than and "before" the individual, just as psychology in the same period speaks of "super-ego" in connection with group pressures against the individuals.[6]

The vocabulary of socialization parallels to an amazing degree the lexicon of political power, as if the names of the hierarchical facts had been changed just to protect everyone's innocence. Once the individual has been brought into a kind of natural or "second-nature" membership,[7] the group "other" than and "before" the individual then becomes "legitimate" or "right" in the member's eyes, without any question being raised about the member's obligation to that group. To raise the issue of obligation would be to question the group's naturalness. Socialization suggests a kind of natural induction into group membership, tied to the biological life cycle. Political socialization, as a field of inquiry, tends to play down the artificiality of such induction.[8]

But, clearly, socialization is very artificial. As a result, individuals can hardly be in any position to exercise independent judgment about what is legitimate political conduct. Instead, they accept as inevitable and universally natural the kind of politics they experience locally. Here "consent of the governed" is no longer consent at all, since the issue of obligation to the local political unit cannot be raised, but becomes instead "the engineering of consent," as a leading student of propaganda once described it.[9] If power concerns domination, then political socialization is admirably suited for the politics of power, because this communications process rules out independent questioning about the problem of political obligation.

Contrasted to political socialization, the second method of political communication appears much more subjective and cosmopolitan. Political education emphasizes above all the artificiality of political order and the citizen as a creative actor within this order. In the history of practical politics there have been only infrequent periods when political education of this sort has triumphed over narrower, more disciplined socialization, most notably, during sporadic intervals in ancient Athens from the fifth-century Sophists to the Hellenist cosmopolitans in the fourth and third centuries B.C.[10] The history of political thought, however, has been stirred by a number of important spokesmen for such education. In fact, as will be argued at the close of this chapter, an open, cosmopolitan view of education lies at the heart of the classical democratic position on civic virtue; not the ideal, omnicompetent citizen (an impossible concept), but the free man armed with enough political sophistication to participate in politics as a person with the capacity for independent judgment, despite the pressures from political socialization. The will to exercise such judgment, however, must be as carefully inculcated as the will to obey blindly the orders of superiors, yet without allowing political education to change into socialization.

Anticipating somewhat a later discussion of "participatory politics," it seems that the politics of participation encourages political education much more than does the politics of power. In the first place, the politics of participation emphasizes the discovery of political values through common action by the entire membership, rather than through the mediation of special authorities. And in the second place, through such common action personal confrontations between large numbers of citizens can take place. While such confrontations may be quite dramatic at times, the result may also be a wider, more cosmopolitan exploration of what it means to be a human being than occurs where hierarchies make such determinations and ordinary citizens mainly defer without seriously questioning their group's views. Confrontations like this would tend to encourage self-development rather than hinder it—providing, of course, that the true spirit of participation were emphasized through education. The aim of such confrontations is not competition for ascendancy, but personal identity for every member.

Questions raised about obligation and consent, therefore, belong to the politics of participation and not to the politics of power. Such issues arise during the course of political education, but not during socialization. The idea, current in political science, that power is a transactional relationship between persons and groups,[11] can be conceived of only in a cultural setting not wholly given to domination and socialization. Not surprisingly, American and British political scientists have led the way on the transactional view of power; indeed, the development of this point of view is very closely linked to the question of democracy's future. Yet it is also no surprise that a political theory dealing with the central problem of obligation, as some have argued is the case with Western political thought,[12] should not develop elsewhere. It is the feature of all despotisms that obligation represents an illicit question raised only on pain of punishment.[13] In addition, the pathos of those in the West who have raised the issue, from Antigone to protesters against the Vietnam War, indicates that participation nearly always occupies a secondary place to power, even when it appears in the open.

From the citizen's subjective vantage point, therefore, the central question is always one of the relationship between participation and power in his culture. This relation is the great problem of citizenship. Democracy and dictatorship, on the other hand, relate to forms of government together with the procedures involved in selecting these governments. Though democracy and dictatorship are obviously connected to participation and power, the first set of relationships more closely parallels the central concern of political leadership, the second that of ordinary citizens. In a very real sense, therefore, there are two types of political theory, that of leadership and that of citizenship. Only Western political thought—with Gandhi's notable exception—has given much sustained attention to the second type, and only Western political societies have had much experience with communications centering on participation by an independent citizenry.

METHODS OF POLITICAL COMMUNICATION
RELATED TO THE POLITICS OF POWER

Why the politics of power should place such disproportionate emphasis on political socialization is an intriguing question. One explanation might be the following. Removal of much valuable political experience means that ordinary citizens will rely for their political information on a hierarchy, if they want information at all. Since leaders are doing truly important things, while ordinary citizens have unimportant political tasks, it follows that knowledge relevant to the most important areas of power politics must flow downward from leaders to citizens. This control of most important political knowledge by leaders constitutes, of course, a very basic element in perpetuating power politics. In other words, a hierarchical group mediates political truth through a structure of power, such group mediation being political socialization. As a result, power and socialization go together.

As social life becomes more complex, subject to a growing "organic division of labor," so brilliantly described by Emile Durkheim in his *The Division of Labor in Society*, the reliance on leadership for important political information becomes even greater, particularly as states attempt, as they all do, to meet complexity with stronger leadership. Thus America's increasingly complicated political problems require an ever more powerful President, it is argued, but this only subjects civic knowledge in the United States all the more to presidential control. Little of political life on the side of actual policy decisions takes place any more within an ordinary citizen's life space, though the execution of these decisions invades his personal life almost daily.[14] Much of life becomes cluttered, therefore, with problems a citizen has no responsibility for initiating or solving. Even for those problems directly related to him, he will more than likely pay deference to his leaders for information and guidance in how he ought to solve them. Without such direction an ordinary citizen may even become paralyzed, for he is alienated from personal action and decision.

It has also been argued, in connection with the dichotomy between power and participation, that participation encourages one form of cultural communication, political education, whereas power encourages another form, political socialization. So obviously where power dominates political culture, as it does most often today, socialization will be the prevailing method of communication from culture to citizen, but not the only method. Political education will appear wherever free citizen participation occurs within the power culture. Hitler's extermination of the Jews, his burning of books, his purging of the arts and universities were all aimed at the area of cosmopolitan, subjective education that totalitarian power cannot abide. Yet even where political education is not so systematically persecuted, very interesting changes take place in this education as it is affected by the power orthodoxy. These changes are parallel to those that take place in participation itself, such as in voting, when participation falls under the influence of power. To preserve the bare outlines of political education, and at the same time communicate meaningfully to indoctrinated citizens in the politics of power, proponents of this education often adopt unwittingly some of the accepted mannerisms of the politics of power. Above all, in the politics of power political education must not incite citizens to independent action, for this is not condoned by the culture, and citizens would probably not understand the real meaning of the incitement in any case. "Objectivity" is the hallmark of political education in the politics of power. Profound thinkers of the past who have participated in a liberal tradition may be "studied," but the subjective passion of their profound thought cannot be communicated. Anyone communicating this passion takes serious liberties with the toleration that power has for him and others like him. Deference must be paid to alienated action and decision: By alienating thought from action, objective knowledge closely resembles voting where citizens may think about political things, but leaders do the acting.

As the politics of power becomes more and more restrictive in the break down of representative democracy, even those areas of individual objectivity, representing symbolically a truer political education, are crushed in the name of group conformity, a process that explains to some extent the totalitarian intolerance for objective knowledge. It is not the individual committed to political truth as he sees it versus dispassionate, objective intellect that is at issue in the struggles between totalitarianism and objectivity, since passionate individual commitment to subjective values is nowhere popular in the politics of power, and least of all in totalitarian settings. Rather, the main contention is between irrational group commitment and an objective political education which is but a pale shadow of true political education, but which still represents that education in the minds of freedom's enemies. Physical scientists are distrusted by totalitarian regimes and by some persons in nontotalitarian contexts, not because science is dispassionate (Adolf Eichmann testified that he dispassionately carried out higher orders to murder millions of people), but because the objectivity that science holds important represents, however imperfectly, the tradition of humanist political education, not the politics of power.

Typical political education in the politics of power concerns learning *about* government and values relating to politics, rather than *practicing* (participating in) government. Learning values, but not carrying out the imperatives of values in action, constitutes "conventional morality" which is what liberal education often becomes in political settings alien to its full development. Associated with objectified humanism is what might be called "conventional liberalism," an objective catalogue of liberal values held by individuals who sporadically, if at all, translate this catalogue into practical action. Useful here is a distinction Hannah Arendt has made between strict "knowledge" about humans and "understanding" of those humans.[15] Education in the context of hierarchical power deals more with knowledge—analytical, logical, objective: Education in participatory situations emphasizes understanding—empathetic wisdom, personal commitment, subjectivity. Since socialization controls methods of communication within the politics of power, it forces a more liberal education (which does not stress disciplined *group* mediation and commitment, but rather *individual* commitment) out of the committed realm entirely into the area of objectivity. Thus, objective sociology considers the dichotomy between individual and group unreal or at most two sides of the same coin, the "I" (self) and "me" (group image of self), in George Herbert Mead's terminology.[16]

On the other hand, Paul Goodman has remarked that while he can appreciate the sociological conception of a social role, he cannot relate this conception to his own life, because he feels so personally dissatisfied with his performance in these roles. From his standpoint, there is obviously conflict between individual and society, because the individual has the subjective experience of playing a role, while society can only "give" the role to the individual.[17]

Yet society not only gives roles to individuals, but also makes them responsible for how they play roles for which they may have serious feelings of inadequacy. Citizenship is a prime example of a stereotyped "given" status, with certain prescribed styles for playing roles within that status, which at the same time demands duties from those privileged enough to occupy this status. Since most citizens are powerless, however, there must be widespread alienation—estrangement—from any real sense of responsibility for how the role is played. Desperate attempts may be made to make something meaningful out of a status largely devoid of a political power that is commensurate with the responsibility which this status requires. Heavy responsibilities remain, however, regardless of feelings of inadequacy.[18]

POLITICAL ROLE

Having discussed the two methods of political communications, it is time to ask what kind of information these communications are meant to convey. Obviously "political communications" communicate political information. But such information varies. The most important question for any citizen is, "What am I to do in my status as a citizen?" In other words, what the citizen needs is a picture of proper action in the form of explicit and more subtle cues about what should be done. This picture can be called, in its sum, a "role." But this image of action, the role, is actually more a jigsaw pattern than a whole cloth; that is, the picture has a number of premises, again more or less explicit and more or less restrictive, about how the role should be played.[19] These premises appear either as "indicatives" (what *is* the case—beliefs) or "imperatives" (what *should be* the case—values).[20] Once cues are taken by the individual citizen as indicatives and imperatives, one can speak of his "taking" the citizen's role.

Exactly how a citizen will play this role depends on two things, on the explicitness of the cues, meaning how unambiguous are the rules (premises) for playing, and on the individual himself. It is convenient, therefore, to distinguish between the actual playing of a role as the "making" of a role by an individual ("role style"), and the role premises he simply is "taking" from his culture. Role taking and role making constitute separate activities, though in extremely restrictive social contexts they may be virtually identical.[21] One vital determinant of how far role taking and role making diverge from each other, and thus how free the citizen will be in improvising his own actions, will be the prevailing methods by which communications about role cues are made from culture to citizen. Political socialization tends to make these cues or premises more explicit, sometimes to the point of severely limiting creative latitude by stereotyping, while political education works to broaden role possibilities (see the following paragraphs). For complicated but discernible reasons the citizen role has been especially subject to such stereotyping. As noted earlier, what the prevailing method of communication will be depends very much on what is the usual emphasis in political culture, participation or power.

No man in social situations is a Robinson Crusoe, least of all in political situations. Cultural transmission of role information is inescapable. In this transmission two crucial variables are present: (*a*) what information is made available (political objects) and (*b*) how it is communicated from culture to citizen (political communications). These two variables, together with individual idiosyncrasies to a lesser degree (since these can be adjusted by political cultures using biological and psychological controls), will determine the ways in which citizens will act.

Through one method of political communication, socialization, the citizen role is taken primarily as a "given," with some eccentricities probable. But the role, not the person, provides the most basic value and belief premises and thus may prove extremely inflexible. Under these circumstances the role runs the risk of becoming stereotyped, played by rote with little conscious evaluation of the role by the actor. This has happened, for instance, where voting is deemed the citizen's main function. When stereotyping is widespread, one finds a nation of unvirtuous citizens who have "habits" of voting—for which the study of "voting behavior" seems appropriate—but no deeper political commitments. True virtue, however, deals with morality, morality with imperatives, imperatives with action, action with intention as well as habitual response. But habit is unintentional and by itself no path to virtue. Habit has other functions, such as social stability, something intentional action can never guarantee.[22] In other words, if "good citizenship" has anything to do with "civic virtue," then habitual socialization is an insufficient guide for citizenship. Political education complements habit by encouraging sound independent judgment on the part of every member not handicapped by below-average native intelligence.

Citizens under the influence of political education have a more independent point of view in directions already indicated. Although political education tends to encourage flexibility in role making, much depends upon the context of that political education. As already argued, political education carried on within the politics of power moves toward objectivity, to a greater or lesser extent depending on the particular politics of power, and in the process discourages an independent point of view based on this education. Such a point of view is largely irrelevant to objective knowledge. Hence the citizen in search of an independent position must move increasingly between group socialization and objective truth, into a valuational gap where alienation seems the only basis for a point of view. The poverty of such alienation for developing a positive set of political values is apparent.

FEEDBACK
FROM CIVIC ACTION TO POLITICAL CULTURE

The fourth and final phase of the political culture model constructed here concerns the effect that the citizen's role playing has on the objective and subjective aspects of political culture. In describing this phase, the expression "feedback" seems especially appropriate. The term is not meant to convey any elaborate notion of politics as a system of communications, for this has already been done in political science by Karl Deutsch and others.[23] But the expression reveals something very useful for the present discussion, since it illustrates well the thesis that the roots of unvirtuous, lazy citizenship are found not in the limitations of individual intelligence and morality but in political activity; or more correctly, individual human nature and political activity are so interrelated that one can deal with their relationships only by employing a closed-system communications model that uses feedback.

By playing his role in a basically unvirtuous style—with little thought to participation—the modern citizen sends back a communication to his political culture, in the form of a cue or role premise for those in power. His message reads: "I have little interest in political matters, consider this disinterest as license for you to move freely about your business of governing, subject to certain minimal controls." For some observers, this apparently universal lack of citizen interest might "prove" that "human nature" is really oriented toward mundane matters of family, income, and leisure, and is not very much concerned about political matters transcending immediate, personal involvements. Something intrinsic seems to drive most persons toward immediate gratifications rather than distant goals; people are limited by intellect and time from following closely political action, which they see as removed from them, distant. For the "larger" issues there exist special, professionalized political cadres. In other words, one could establish a seemingly sound argument that ordinary human beings have basic survival uppermost in their minds (and hearts), and politics is thus apt to appear rather remote for most persons. Since through the ages, with very few exceptions, man has been ruled by hierarchies, there would seem to be historical confirmation about his basically unpolitical nature. But this assumption is weak, for the message the citizen sends to his culture of power may really be a socially conditioned response to a three-part message already transmitted by that culture to him since his early youth: "The proper political order is one of governors and governed, leaders and led, elite and nonelite. Man needs hierarchical authority for social peace. The centers for this authority, and for the vital decisions made by this authority in society's name, are remote from you." The politics of power has persisted through the ages. Who is the ordinary citizen, born under some hierarchy at some minute point in time, to question it?

There have been, of course, exceptions taken to the notion that most people have little interest in politics. Participatory political culture has expanded and contracted in every nation's history. And much attention has been paid to the subject of civic virtue in the history of political theory. These exceptions should lead one to doubt, perhaps, the generalization that ordinary citizens are *by nature* unpolitical, especially when one also takes into account that politics is itself a cultural, man-made phenomenon.

The evidence suggests that: (1) Basic human nature is not responsible for a society ruled by power—there is nothing absent in the human potential that necessitates an unvirtuous, slothful citizenry dominated by hierarchical power; (2) the limits of human nature in this regard are established by political culture with its prevailing objects for attention, its methods of communication, and its accepted ways for playing the citizen's role; and (3) citizens react within the limits specified, thus reinforcing these limits in a closed circle of stimulus, response, and feedback to stimulus, response, feedback, and so on.

Some citizens manage to break out of this closed system—the contemporary revolt of some young Americans against "the system" seems symptomatic of this breaking out—but all depends upon the amount and quality of political education available. Generally, citizens have merely challenged and overthrown one system of power and replaced it with another ("The King is dead, long live the King"), with perhaps a short space between hierarchies for political experimentation. Overwhelming historical evidence indicates a normal human pattern which encourages the politics of power. But exceptions both in practice and in the history of political thought, where proponents of civic virtue along participatory lines are quite prominent, are more important here, for by their very existence these exceptions suggest that slothful citizenship is only a feedback response from a prevailing culture, a response which in turn reinforces that culture. What is sometimes taken as the *cause* of the politics of power, the unpolitical nature of ordinary citizens, turns out to be an *effect* of the politics of power and one which further reinforces this politics.

How the few powerful ever gained the ascendancy presents a fascinating enigma. But surely it has as much, if not more, to do with the force and skill of leaders, as it has with the "need" people have for political order, even while they exhibit only trifling concern for that order. (The classic work on this topic is Rousseau's *Discourse on the Origins of Inequality*.) How can anyone *not* be deeply concerned about political decisions, such as thermonuclear war, that affect one's life and family? But what can be done, by the ordinary citizen in the politics of power, to influence these basic decisions? What direct, immediate power does he have? And without effective power, why should he register any *apparent* concern? No wonder ordinary citizens care little about politics when the most basic decisions of all, those dealing with life and death matters, are made in the utmost secrecy among councils of war, lest *we* inform our enemies. Yet, if the ordinary citizen is not allowed into these councils, is not he too the enemy? Which do the leaders of a nation fear most as they talk in secrecy, other nations or their own citizens? It is a peculiar politics which takes the questions most vital to citizens and decides these questions in the most secret places away from citizens. This secrecy cannot be justified on any grounds except the politics of power, whether the question involves international war or maintaining the hierarchy in the face of citizen participation. Such secrecy on the most vital questions affecting citizens presents the great contemporary paradox. This paradox requires an urgent and satisfactory solution in favor of that civic virtue associated with participatory politics, for hinging on the solution may be the preservation of mankind itself. Only through a politics of participation can the interests of the great mass of "mankind" be heard at all.

CONCLUSION:
THE DEMOCRATIC THEORISTS AND CIVIC VIRTUE

In conclusion, the effects of the three subjective phases of political culture on citizenship reinforce greatly the effects of objective political culture. Methods of communication, related to power politics, tend to overemphasize leader-follower relationships and the social discipline connected with such relationships. Role playing under these circumstances is much more stereotyped than it would be under participatory politics and political education. Citizen response in the politics of power moves in a feedback direction to the political culture, tending to reinforce established hierarchical patterns in a closed system of stimulus and response. It becomes evident that the psychological language of stimulus-response conditioning, when applied to politics at least, becomes part of the vocabulary of power, just as the engineering language of communications and systems, when transferred to political considerations, contributes to the same vocabulary (actually both stimulus-response and communications systems are already power vocabularies in their original fields). The conduct of citizens in the culture of power is basically unvirtuous in that it has little to do with the citizen's main duty as an agent responsible for common participation based on independent points of view, eventually fostering that mutual responsibility which alone enriches the commonwealth's life.

As it sees everything else in power terms, the culture of political power also reads into the history of political theory a politics of power. No one can deny that hierarchy and power figure prominently in this history, but neither can one deny that some important theorists have given attention to participation's impact on civic virtue. The lack of interest in power is especially true of certain democratic thinkers who have concerned themselves less with how nonleaders might "control" leaders[24] and more with developing a commonwealth where large numbers of persons might participate on an equal footing in making important political decisions, thus perfecting their own development as well as their community's. When one reads the famous Putney Debates between Cromwell's Independent leaders and the Leveller representatives in the Puritan Army in seventeenth-century England, one catches a glimpse of the continuous confrontation between power and participation in the history of political theory. For as they argued for the right of the "poorest he" to have equal voice in political affairs with the "richest he," the Leveller representatives were trying to point out to Cromwell's spokesmen that the hierarchical imperatives involved in organizing and governing a state must be balanced by the participatory imperatives involved in creating a free, virtuous people. As the debates wore on, it became evident to those in power, Cromwell and his elite, that power and participation did not mix. But this was not the Leveller position, for they were not anarchists opposing power per se, even though the Independents sensed anarchy in their demands. Rather, the Levellers argued for the compatibility of participation and power and for the *balance* of these two forms of politics, an argument which is also the position of this essay. Many of the powerful can never see the justice of this position, for they are basically interested in an unvirtuous citizenry, slothful in its habits of participation and only too glad to pass the burdens of government to leaders.

When one examines other democratic theorists besides the dauntless Levellers, for example, the work of Rousseau, de Tocqueville, T. H. Green, and Dewey, one finds the same insistence on redressing the balance between power and participation in the name of civic virtue. In all four cases there is little or no interest in the institutions of political power, except as they affect citizen interest in participation. Each theorist is concerned with civic virtue among ordinary citizens, and each identifies this virtue with the kind of participatory politics and political education mentioned earlier in this chapter. None of these four, and surely not the Levellers, believed in that unicorn, the omnicompetent average citizen. But each did believe that citizens could strengthen their independent judgment and thus their civic virtue through responsible, common participation in making crucial political decisions as well as by simply voting for leaders.

This interest in civic virtue in the form of common participation helps explain Rousseau's communitarian solution to the problem he posed early in *The Social Contract*, "to find a form of association which will defend and protect with the whole common force the person and goods of each associate, and in which each, while uniting himself with all, may still obey himself alone and remain as free as before."[25] The politics of power, Rousseau argued earlier in his *Discourse on the Origins of Inequality*, has corrupted citizens to the point where they may have lost sight of what it means to be free, perhaps even to where they have become alienated from any semblance of political virtue. The fear that such alienation had already taken place explains Rousseau's cryptic recommendation in *The Social Contract* that, given the meaninglessness of civic virtue, men may have to be "forced" into freedom. Force exercised in the name of virtue represents the philosophy of certain theorists in the French Revolution, not that of Rousseau, but it does symbolize Rousseau's pessimistic view that the citizen had vanished. Since the really free man was no more a reality, Rousseau proposed to deal with him as one might the extinct saber-toothed tiger, a creature from the prehistoric past—Rousseau's famous state of nature—of which one can only reconstruct an imaginative model based on certain fossilized remains available to us. The free citizen may be as extinct as the saber-tooth, represented today only by certain ancient relics in symbolic forms, like "participation," and in stirring rhetoric as in Pericles' Funeral Oration, but all irrelevant to the realities of power. Given the extinction of the truly free man, Rousseau compromised in favor of a balance between power and participation in the hopes of reconstituting some measure of civic virtue for citizens. But perhaps the notion of civic virtue, however modest in scope, belongs in the same forest primeval with the free man, making the quest for virtue as utopian as reviving those strange prehistoric monsters now calcified in peatbogs and mummified in museums. Nevertheless, Rousseau threw down the political gauntlet in which the measure of humanity will be assessed: "The human savage and civilized [*policé*] man so differ, at base of heart and inclinations. . .that the supreme happiness of one would reduce the other to despair."[26] It is part of Rousseau's genius that he saw *the problem of human identity tied to the subject of citizenship*, a point this essay will return to in Chapter 5.

Notes to Chapter 3

1. A distinction should be made between "role" and "status." See Ralph Linton, *The Study of Man* (New York: Appleton-Century-Crofts, 1936), pp. 113–114.

2. A basic treatment of "political socialization" is found in Herbert Hyman, *Political Socialization*, (New York: The Free Press, 1959). This work includes the following premise which Hyman considers "self-evident": ". . .*humans must learn their political behavior early and well and persist in it*. Otherwise there would be no regularity—perhaps even chaos" (p. 17). The emphasis is Hyman's.

3. Contemporary socialization studies show some remarkable parallels to the thinking of William Graham Sumner in his *Folkways* (1906).

4. Charles E. Merriam's important contribution to the study of citizenship is found in his *The Making of Citizens* (Chicago: University of Chicago, 1931).

5. See Gabriel Almond and Sidney Verba, *The Civic Culture* (Princeton, N. J.: Princeton University Press, 1963) Part 3, chapter 12, on types of political socialization.

6. The terminology of nineteenth- and twentieth-century sociology mentioned here is evident in a basic book of readings collected by Robert E. Park and Ernest W. Burgess, *Introduction to the Science of Sociology* (Chicago: University of Chicago Press, 1924), pp. 64–160.

7. Johann Gottlieb Fichte, as quoted by Lord Haldane, in Park and Burgess, pp. 106–107.

8. See Hannah Arendt's comments on the relationship of the behavioral sciences to contemporary interest in the biological life cycle, *The Human Condition* (New York: Doubleday & Company, Inc., 1958) pp. 292–297.

9. On the engineering of consent, see Edward L. Bernays, *Propaganda* (1928), cited in Stanley Kelley, Jr., *Public Relations and Political Power* (Baltimore: The Johns Hopkins Press, 1956), p. 229. A good statement against such manipulation may be found in Christian Bay, *The Structure of Freedom* (Stanford, Calif.: Stanford University Press, 1958).

10. Jacob Burckhardt's narrow view of politics as power led him to describe the Athenian experience as a victory of "culture" over "politics." See his *Force and Freedom*, ed. by James Hastings Nichols (New York: Meridian Books, Inc., 1955), pp. 188–204. Compare his treatment of Athens to that of Werner Jaeger in *Paideia, The Ideals of Greek Culture* (Oxford: Basil Blackwell & Mott, Ltd., 1954).

11. The transactional view of power is "spelled out" in Harold D. Lasswell and Abraham Kaplan, *Power and Society* (New Haven, Conn.: Yale University Press, 1950), Part 2, chapter 5.

12. The view of Charles E. McIlwain, *The Growth of Political Thought in the West* (New York: Crowell-Collier and Macmillan, Inc., 1932), p. 1.

13. Note the anxieties of various interests in Oriental despotism: The ruler can trust no one, the official is eternally suspicious, and the commoner has fear of being involved. Karl Wittfogel, *Oriental Despotism* (New Haven, Conn.: Yale University Press, 1959), pp. 155–156.

14. On the idea of "life space," see Kurt Lewin, *Field Theory in Social Science*, ed. by Dorwin Cartwright (New York: Harper and Row, Publishers, 1964), pp. 43–59.

15. For Hannah Arendt's distinction between knowledge and understanding, see her "Understanding and Politics," *Partisan Review*, 20 (July–August 1953), 377–392; and her "Politics and Truth," *The New Yorker*, XLIII (February 25, 1967), 49–88.

16. On the "I" and "me," see George Herbert Mead, *Mind, Self and Society*, ed. by Charles W. Morris (Chicago: University of Chicago Press, 1934), pp. 173–178.

17. See Paul Goodman, *Utopian Essays and Practical Proposals* (New York: Alfred A. Knopf, 1964), pp. 110–118.

18. Consider for a moment who bears the responsibility for wars which represent the breakdown of negotiations between a few persons. Attention is called to the quotation from Hannah Arendt's *Eichmann in Jerusalem* (New York: The Viking Press, Inc., 1963), p. 255, which is at the beginning of Chapter 5. The German nation bore responsibility for murdering the Jews, Miss Arendt insists, but she also adds that Eichmann, *as an individual*, shared in this responsibility.

19. The idea of "role premise" has been adapted from Herbert A. Simon's concept of "decision premise," which is set forth in *Administrative Behavior*, 2d ed. (New York: Crowell-Collier and Macmillan, Inc., 1957), p. xxxii and elsewhere in his writings.

20. For further discussion of "indicative" and "imperative," see R. M. Hare, *The Language of Morals*, (Oxford: Oxford University Press, 1952), Part 1.

21. The distinction between role taking and role making can be found in Ralph Turner, "Role-Taking: Process versus Conformity," in Arnold Rose, ed., *Human Behavior and Social Processes* (London: Routledge & Kegan Paul Ltd., 1962), chapter 2. See also the distinction between "behavior" and "experience" developed by Ronald D. Laing, *The Politics of Experience* (New York: Pantheon Books, Inc., 1967), chapter 1.

22. On intention, virtue, and conventional morality, see Hare, Part 2, chapter 9. Aristotle saw virtue as both habitually conditioned (*ethos*) and consciously exercised, but apparently did not detect possible tensions between these two views. For example, see his *Nicomachean Ethics*, Books 2 and 3. A sophisticated discussion of these tensions, by a contemporary ethical philosopher, may be found in Dorothy Emmet, *Rules, Roles and Relations* (New York: St. Martin's Press, Inc., 1966), chapters 7–9. For views in some ways similar to the one presented here, and also stressing "rules" much as Dorothy Emmet does, see Peter Winch's distinction between "habit" and "rule" in *The Idea of a Social Science* (London: Routledge & Kegan Paul Ltd., 1958), chapter 2; and Robert J. Pranger, "An Explanation for Why Final Authority Is Necessary," *American Political Science Review*, LX (December 1966), 994–997.

23. For use of communications terminology in contemporary political science theory, see Karl Deutsch, *The Nerves of Government* (New York: The Free Press, 1963).

24. The problem of "controlling" leaders as the central question facing modern democracies has been explored by Robert A. Dahl and Charles E. Lindblom, *Politics, Economics and Welfare* (New York: Harper and Row, Publishers, 1963), Part 4, chapters 10–11, in their concept of "polyarchy"; and by Dahl in *A Preface to Democratic Theory* (Chicago: University of Chicago Press, 1956), chapter 3, in his notion of polyarchal democracy. See also Almond and Verba, pp. 180ff; and Peter Bachrach's juxtaposition of the theory of democratic elitism and classical democratic theory in *The Theory of Democracy Elitism, A Critique* (Boston: Little, Brown & Company, 1967), p. 100.

25. See Jean Jacques Rousseau, *The Social Contract* (1762), Book 1, chapter 6.

26. *Discours sur l'inégalité*, Seconde Partie, in *Jean Jacques Rousseau, The Political Writings*, ed. by C. E. Vaughan (Oxford: Basil Blackwell & Mott, Ltd., 1962), Vol. I, p. 195.

Chapter 4

A HISTORICAL AND SOCIOLOGICAL EXAMI-
NATION OF THE DEMOCRATIC PROCESS,
WHETHER LEADING TO ITS REVERSAL IN
TOTAL RULE OR TO THE REALIZATION OF ITS
IDEA, IS JUST A STEP TO GET OUR BEARINGS.
THE KNOWLEDGE WE GAIN MUST AWAKEN
OUR OWN IMPULSES. THE QUESTION IS
WHAT THE CRITIC WANTS, OR WHETHER HE
WANTS NOTHING.

Karl Jaspers
The Future of Mankind

. . .THE NATURE OF HIM I OBEY SIGNIFIES
LESS TO ME THAN THE FACT OF EXTORTED
OBEDIENCE.

De Tocqueville
Democracy in America

"PARTICIPATION" IS NOT AN ALTERNATIVE
TO "DELEGATION" BUT SEEMS, RATHER, TO
PROTECT IT AGAINST DEGENERATING INTO
"ABDICATION."

Joseph Tussman
Obligation and the Body Politic

4

Representative Democracy as a Politics of Power

The vanishing citizen, whose rightful role is to create a politics of participation but who is no longer capable of doing so, may seem a far cry from the apparent allegiance some contemporary political cultures display for the free citizen. American politics places heavy accent on civic participation, does it not? Opinion surveys reveal that Americans tend to be participation-minded, holding this high among the list of what they consider values of good citizenship. One study of five nations, Germany, Great Britain, Italy, Mexico, and the United States, by Gabriel Almond and Sidney Verba of Stanford University, places the United States at the top of the five in terms of its citizens' concern for political participation.[1] A UNESCO survey on the meaning of "democracy" in the late 1940s, an ambitious exercise in semantic clarification of a difficult political expression, showed that countries outside the Iron Curtain area saw democracy mainly in terms of "government *by* the people," while nations in the Soviet orbit preferred democracy as "government by an elite *for* the people."[2] Again, the accent in the United States was on popular participation. Finally, countless textbooks,

61

pamphlets, and hortative speeches on "good citizenship" in the United States commend citizen participation as a special virtue.

In contrast to this allegiance to participative values noted among Americans and to a lesser extent among others, studies of American voting behavior usually draw unflattering profiles of the ordinary citizen's electoral competence. Habitual responses clearly overrule rational calculations.[3] If one identifies voting with widespread civic participation, the equation most generally made,[4] then participation is honored more in the breach than in practice. Furthermore, any kind of civic activity other than voting is largely undertaken by a rather small band of "activists" and "influentials."[5] Discount for the moment voting's importance, even for democracies, and consider whether the value that Americans supposedly attach to political participation does not resemble those *Saturday Evening Post* covers which used to evoke a nostalgia nowhere replicated in contemporary life.

The role of participation in representative democracy, particularly the question of voting's importance, will be explored in the first sections of this chapter. One of the most time-tested formulas in political science concerns the obsolescence of direct democracy. According to this formula, today's large and complicated societies can be popularly governed only through representative institutions buttressed by bureaucratic expertise.[6] He who says democracy, means representation, although the opposite is not always the case. Through a marriage of convenience, leadership (power) and citizenship (participation) have been joined together in representative democracy. If one adheres to the distinction between power and participation, the results of this marriage are worth exploring from the standpoint of citizenship as well as from the outlook of leadership. The question of how the citizen is constricted in his political decisions by representation is at least as important as how the representative is constrained in his choices, though political scientists concentrate almost entirely on the latter problem.

After having discussed representation in relation to participation, representation as one form of the politics of power will then be examined in its relation to oligarchy, another form of power. Growing evidence indicates that not only has the representative partnership allowed leadership to dominate citizenship by creating expanded political distances between leaders and led, but oligarchy is now undermining even the outward trappings of ideal representative democracy, where participation has a symbolic, if not a tangible, place. From the citizen's perspective the trend is toward more stringent forms of power than representation, forms not easily controlled within traditional constitutional restraints. An explanation for such a trend will conclude this chapter.

REPRESENTATIVE DEMOCRACY

Representation raises some thorny questions both in political thought and action, going to the heart of such matters as authority and law. But the basic legal principle behind representative government seems fairly clear: Representatives, however invested with the power they possess, are authorized in advance to act jointly in behalf of their constituents and to bind them by their collective decisions. As noted in Chapter 1, this principle is known as *plena potestas*. This principle was utilized in law as far back as the ancient Roman emperors and early popes, but it was developed as the basis for legislative institutions with collective memberships only in the late Middle Ages. Important for present purposes are two aspects of this basic principle, that of special, plenary authority binding constituents to what their representatives decide according to previously established procedures, and that of collective, collegial decision making by the representative body. The feature of authority indicates that representative institutions belong in the politics of power, while the collective aspect—so suspect in Rousseau's eyes—directs attention to the collegial nature of such power. Both special aspects of the basic representative principle tend to separate leaders from ordinary citizens (the constituents), and extraordinary steps prove necessary to link representatives to their public in relations of mutual responsibility.

The history of representation immediately after the founding of corporate representative institutions in late medieval Europe (almost simultaneously in England, France, and Spain around the turn of the fourteenth century) was one of constitutionalism, that is, the attempts by parliamentary bodies to share power with strong national monarchs. Delegates to the early Parliaments in fourteenth- and fifteenth-century England could hardly be called "popular" leaders, since they had little contact in any regular form with a mass electorate. Nor were they at first much more than the king's agents, essential for raising funds for monarchical adventures but by no means independent shareholders in political power. Born as instruments of power, and in spite of their later democratization, representative institutions still bear the stamp of power. The evolution of the English Parliament, together with the parallel demise of its sister institutions in France and Spain, is a familiar story. By the seventeenth century the English Parliament, banded together as a body of colleagues, had moved into conflict with the monarchy, finally ending a century-long struggle with victories in the Glorious Revolution of 1688 and the Act of Settlement in 1701. During this same period absolutism won the day in France and Spain.

As early as the seventeenth century, leaders of the Leveller party during the English Revolution advocated more popular links between representatives and people, for during Parliament's ascendancy its membership represented oligarchic England. Though Leveller demands for nearly universal manhood suffrage and annual parliaments were not revived again until the Chartists two centuries later, the position that participation should counterbalance power (mentioned in Chapter 3 in reference to the Levellers) was part of English political culture—if only a minor part—by the time true democratization of Parliament began in the mid-nineteenth century. This process of democratization in England continued until 1948 when plural voting for seats in the House of Commons was abolished (certain university graduates from Cambridge and Oxford had been allowed an extra vote for parliamentary members from special constituencies established for those universities). In essence, the Levellers demanded that representation be made more democratic by linking leaders and led through periodic elections involving large numbers of persons from many different classes.

As known today, therefore, representative democracy results from the confluence of two forces, the practice of representation with ancient roots and late medieval efflorescence, and the ancient idea of popular democracy, in its Puritan revival and nineteenth-century effulgence in America and Europe. These two forces, specific to the history of representation, have been joined by a third political force in the twentieth century, administrative organization, a force that has added even more oligarchic overtones to contemporary democracy. The first force represents the politics of power; the second force, under proper conditions, the politics of participation; the third force, a strengthening of power. Both the first force and the third have also been connected with advancing professionalization that adds distance between leaders and led.

Popular representative institutions have proved a fairly efficient way for governing large numbers of persons across extensive geographical distances. In addition to their constitutional and democratic functions, therefore, these institutions have been justified as the only adequate means for governing most states. This justification was displayed prominently in Madison's arguments in *The Federalist*. The authors of these pamphlets advocating ratification of the new American Constitution in 1787 also argued that representative government, by dividing the nation into geographical constituencies, would tend to fragment national majorities, thus saving the country from majority tyranny. Here then were arguments that joined efficiency with freedom, an almost peerless combination. Unfortunately, the participatory aspect of democracy, where a people spontaneously combines to force through governmental measures which are considered urgent by the majority, was sacrificed. Hamilton and Madison mistakenly thought these aspects to be "mob rule," and so have countless Americans in succeeding generations who prefer their constitutional "republic" to "democracy."

Along with establishing an electoral link between representatives and citizens, other issues have arisen concerning the "proper" form for representative democracy. One question, the kind of constituency, has been traditionally resolved in favor of geographical patterns of representation; men represent districts or constituencies of people grouped according to lines on maps. Opposition to this dominant geographical tendency has usually insisted on a more socially organic constituency, such as an occupational group—the theory of corporative representation.

Another question concerns how, once in office, the representative is to behave toward his constituents. Should he act simply as a spokesman for his constituency in obedience to prevailing winds of public opinion, or should he act in the "best interests" of his district even though his actions may not accord with popular pressures? In actual behavior, the representative usually acts *both* ways, though with more emphasis on one than on the other style.[7] But various theories of representation still argue for one of the two positions, and even for other views.

Another kind of issue about democratic representation concerns obligation, a problem especially acute where power and participation have been joined. If one agrees that the representative is empowered to make decisions on one's behalf, does it follow that one must always obey these decisions, even when they conflict with self-interest or with one's sense of justice? When the representative is a powerful monarch or an oligarchic legislative body or both, the issue can always be resolved in the following manner: We, as members of the great mass of ordinary citizens, never empowered or gave authority in any official, explicit manner to these "representatives." Such was the argument of the French Revolution as it spread its doctrines outside France, challenging the legitimacy of princes throughout Europe in the name of popular consent, the rights of man, and the citizen. The argument could be countered rather ineffectively by the idea of the "divine right" of kings to rule. Or sounder notions of tacit approval might provide rejoinders. Or perhaps oligarchic power could be justified on the grounds that in the distant past an actual contract between king and subjects had been transacted and had then become part of the traditional political culture binding all citizens. The divine rights argument had a bogus sound in the face of a democratic ideology which insisted the common people were God's annointed. The second notion of tacit consent proved too much, for any resistance which refused to share in the blessings bestowed by monarchy became *ipso facto* a refutation of the tacit agreement. And the third view of a historical contract, binding future generations as part of a traditional political culture, whatever its descriptive accuracy, rested on the shifting sands of generational differences. Politics involves changing relations over time between power and participation, though seldom if ever giving participation the ascendancy, and thus as the traditional balances are upset, subjects may be released from obligation. Revolution is a case in point of such change, but less dramatic changes within prevalent political interests, such as newly ascendant economic classes, can adversely affect traditional arrangements as well.

Much more potent a means for establishing authority and then fixing civic obligation to that authority has been the electoral tie between leader and led. Once the majority decides, goes the argument, all are legally bound. Democratic practice has constantly refined this notion so as to make obligation under its political system relatively airtight. Some of the refinements have been the following. First, there must be meaningful competition among candidates and issues (usually represented by political parties), so that real choice proves possible. Second, this choice should be uncoerced. Third, all men and women above a certain age should have the right to vote, thus preventing any adult minority from disavowing obligation because it cannot vote. Fourth, the right to vote has become increasingly protected by legal safeguards, a protection only now gaining firm security in the United States. Fifth, each vote must count equally—one man, one vote—so that the concepts of majority and minority are indisputable on strictly numerical grounds. And sixth, the right of minorities to be heard and to be consulted before and after final majority decisions—the princple of opposition—has also been advocated and protected, though rather imperfectly. With all these safeguards, it might be said that representative democracy provides an almost impregnable fortress for the authority of representatives, amounting in some instances perhaps to "tyranny of the majority" or "democratic despotism."

The potent force of representative democracy clearly puts this governmental form within the politics of power, with the added feature of electoral competition that involves large numbers of persons in participatory actions on special occasions. As long as the participatory area can intrude itself into the area of vital decisions, one can speak of some balance between power and participation. Where participation becomes irrelevant to the most vital decisions, then the politics of power has clearly won the day. The latter exigency is now occurring everywhere, even within the context of representative democracy. But in order to see present realities, one must have in mind conditions under which one can speak of participatory politics being encouraged rather than hampered by representative democracy, that is, of participation intruding into the making of crucial decisions. The next section will deal with the latter, more ideal circumstances, together with some contemporary realities within representative democracies which ostensibly encourage participation but which in fact tend to eliminate it.

THE PREREQUISITES
FOR WIDESPREAD CIVIC PARTICIPATION
WITHIN REPRESENTATIVE DEMOCRACY

Democratic community myths support civic participation as *a* prime, if not *the* primary political value. In representative democracies this participation chiefly takes the form of voting for representatives. Also, voting provides the main political cement, the strongest bond of obligation, between governors and governed in democracies. Thus, while such democracies are forms of power politics, the importance of voting is obvious, and where the mass of ordinary citizens participate in such voting, the importance of popular participation is also obvious. But the meaningfulness of the vote in controlling leaders and in providing a place for participatory politics within the arenas of power depends very much on the political culture in which voting occurs. Voting may be competitive, equal and so forth, but still relatively meaningless in terms of how it affects political objects and how it satisfies political expectations among citizens.

What then are the conditions under which representative democracy encourages participation in general, and voting as a form of participation in particular? To answer this question satisfactorily, four related political variables relevant to the participatory functions of representative democracy, "distance," "space," "communication," and "choice," seem useful. Since the third variable, communication, has been covered fully in Chapter 3, it will receive less attention than the others at this point.

The first variable in making representative democracy more congenial for participation, *distance* between governors and governed, usually is taken to mean geographical separation of representatives and constituents. For example, representative government may be rationalized as the only possible government for large territorial states, since the old direct democracy, town-meeting model of direct popular participation proves entirely inappropriate under these conditions. But much more important than geographical expanses is the distance created by the political objects and subjective expectations of a political culture. This kind of distance represents more a symbolic than a physical problem. Where political actors are extraordinary personages, such as Roman emperors and perhaps American Presidents, one can speak of great distances separating leaders and led. In other situations, where leaders walk freely among their people, as a British prime minister must do when he goes to his constituency at election time, one notes the short distance between officials and citizens. Both cases have more to do with symbolic differences than geographic separations. Professional politics, technological changes and massive populations also add to this symbolic distance.

Regarding distance in subjective political culture, an indifference between leaders and led frequently develops in the politics of power. The citizen *feels* "distant," "estranged," "remote," and "powerless" in political life. Here again the separation of government from citizen concerns symbolic meanings attached to relationships much more than territorial separation. True, a citizen living in Los Angeles may feel remote from the President residing in Washington, D. C., but how much of this has to do with geographical distance? So might an unemployed laborer living in the District of Columbia feel equally remote from the President. Faculty colleagues in universities talk about feeling powerless in dealing with campus bureaucracies, yet geographical distance is seldom an issue. Distance is more likely connected with symbolic estrangement—problems of meaning—between followers and centers of power; a separation both objective, as in belonging to economic classes with little or no power (Michael Harrington speaks of the American poor as "out of sight," distant), and subjective, as in socialization patterns that stress government's remoteness.[8] Political analysts are used to a "politics of interest," but here, even within the culture of power, is a "politics of noninterest."

One political factor that contributes greatly to the remoteness of government is war. Participatory politics, which seems to encourage subjective freedom, and cosmopolitan awareness, cannot be reconciled with the politics of war. In all cases, war contradicts the basic values of participation and political education by accentuating the contrary morality of discipline and narrow patriotism. An atmosphere of war, experienced by America for over twenty-five years, has no doubt encouraged rigid political socialization and feelings of abstract objectivity, especially objectivity from one's own allegiance to life-giving forces. The idea of a constant "enemy" stimulates—indeed requires—an alienation from humanity, for one must kill this enemy. Death, not life, becomes the paramount value.[9]

More congenial to participation would be political situations shortening symbolic distances between representatives and constitutents, if not entirely obliterating them. One important reform would be deemphasizing

hierarchical structures throughout society; the idea of "high" governmental officials symbolizes extreme distances. The ideal of constitutional
government that both empowers governments to act and also divides
power into jurisdictions in order to restrain action tends to encourage
separation of leaders and led. In order to decrease distance, constitutionalism should be reexamined, not as a harmful restraint on government, but
as a means for increasing governmental power through compartmentalization. This reassessment would *only* aim to diminish the "height" of
hierarchies, however, not to remove all restraints on government. Another
reform would be greater egalitarianism in order to uplift social classes now
"out of sight." A third factor contributing to shorter symbolic distances
would be deemphasis of conflict values and emphasis on cooperation.
Connected with this new emphasis would be a diminution of tensions with
a view to outlawing war. This change would especially diminish what has
been appropriately called "the veil of secrecy" between leaders and led
today. The symbolism of a "veil" again relates to our distance variable,
just as the veil before the Holy of Holies in the ancient Hebrew tabernacle
signified the enormous distance between God and man. By eliminating much
secrecy, social inequality, and hierarchical aloofness, decreased distance
between representatives and constituents would work to give the voter a
more informed, hence more meaningful basis for choice. Also, the ordinary citizen would move closer to officials and thus intrude his own
judgments into important decision-making processes, a proximity to government which might stimulate more direct forms of civic participation
as well as voting.

The issue here is not *more* citizen access to a remote government along
the lines, for instance, of progressivist programs for initiative, ref-
erendum, and recall procedures, but an improved *quality* of citizen participation. The latter problem requires that the symbolic distance
between leaders and led be cut, not that citizens attempt to bridge an
ever-widening chasm by acting as leaders (the gist of progressivist
proposals).

A second variable for participation within democracy is *space*. This
refers to the amount of room, in relative terms, given participation and
power within a political culture. It has been noted already that the expan-
siveness or space of participation varies over time, seldom in history actually dominating politics, but frequently making some impact in the
fields of political thought and action. As with the idea of distance, space
is used here as a symbolic expression for common meanings shared by
groups of persons. Where the prevalent view of politics shared by citizens
is hierarchical, one might refer to a "political space of power," and
where the view is participatory, one can speak of a "political space of

participation."[10] In most cultures both spaces exist, but the "mores" or prevailing meanings attributed to politics move in power's favor; in other words, the space provided in politics for exercise of power has much more room than that provided for participation. As greater and greater attention focuses on the power factor, participatory space is "squeezed" or constricted still further, until finally, as in Hitler's case, a final triumph of power occurs (symbolized in the famous Nazi propaganda film, *Triumph of the Will,* meaning "the will to power").

Where participation receives true encouragement from representative democracy, a stable or expanding participatory space develops. This situation hardly exists in contemporary democracies. Again, the impact of war and technological change have important repercussions, for the practice of discipline associated with warfare and modern technology provide little space for popular participation, though there is disciplined participation.[11]

An interesting example of how distance and space relate to improved participation in democracy comes from the Israeli army. The new state of Israel, dedicated to participatory politics in both theory and practice, has been forced by its Middle Eastern position to develop a powerful standing army as well. While retaining the discipline of military life, however, the Israelis have attempted to reduce distance within military ranks by curtailing caste distinctions among officer and noncommissioned groups. Although these measures have not met with unqualified success, they do illustrate the sensitivity of Israeli political leadership to the need of some balance between participation and power, to the workings of the related variables of distance and space in achieving this balance, and to the threat of constant military readiness to participatory politics, unless properly counteracted. On the debit side, however, this same leadership has shown less sensitivity to the extensive bureaucratization of Israeli civilian life.

The third variable, *communication*, needs only cursory discussion at this point. Earlier, a distinction was made between two kinds of political communications, socialization and education. At the same time socialization was related to power, and education to participation. Obviously, if political distances are to be diminished and political spaces readjusted, more effort must be devoted to political education as a form of communication. Particularly must greater development of subjective decision making within this education be stressed, instead of concentrating on objective political knowledge. War again has its impact, for the principal theme of warfare is death, not life. The constant fear of death—represented in premonitions about world-wide nuclear disaster, the violent death of loved ones, and the tragedy of millions of young persons cut off from life at the beginnings of their power—hardly provides fertile soil for developing the positive life values associated with political education. These premonitions stem, instead, from feelings of an attenuated responsibility for life, feelings which provide very insecure ground for the moral values of political education.

The fourth and final variable affecting participation is *choice*. Only meaningful choices by an electorate encourage true responsibility of leaders to followers. Where choice resolves into competing, synthetic images of persons running for elective office, electoral choice cannot be meaningful, even if competition exists. A choice with meaning is one where the voter can follow his candidates into public office and affect their policy decisions. Some might argue that the latter case, affecting policy decisions, is accomplished by voters as members of plural interest groups rather than strictly as voters, and thus democracy is preserved. This argument has certain flaws to be discussed later. If the only choice an electorate has is between competing images, more illusory than real— as seems the case today[12]—with no impact on policy formation at all, then the distance between leaders and led is great, the space of participation is small, and the prevailing political communications are objective communiqués rather than subjectively relevant messages. War presents a great problem here too, for a meaningful choice is one where all issues come out into the open, public arena. This presumes that there are no secrets. But warfare encourages secretiveness, and constant war builds secrecy into the institutions of government as an almost traditional way of doing things. The study of elections as the study of crucial decision choices, therefore, cannot ignore those international conflicts that provide settings for these choices, nor neglect the political traditions of secrecy that mature under conditions of permanent war.

If one examines contemporary realities for participation in terms of the four variables just discussed, a less than ideal picture appears. Everywhere, with few exceptions, politics is distant both geographically and culturally. Geographical representation has proved obsolete, forcing nations to adjust the system to new realities. Particularly important has been the rise of corporative representation through formal social and economic councils (France), informal consultations between state officials and private interests (in British economic planning and American lobbying), control of political parties by special interests (slowly but surely taking place in Great Britain), and even regular parliamentary representation (in Ireland and earlier in Fascist Italy). Along with these practical changes have come novel theories of representation which argue for governmental forms more closely connected to modern pluralistic societies.

More impressive than the defaulting of geographical representation, however, has been an increase in cultural distance between representatives and governed. Strong leadership to solve today's complex problems is everywhere advocated. This has meant a decline in traditional representative institutions and the growth of other leadership forms even more distant from participation by ordinary citizens, though not more distant in terms of the impact of their policies on private lives. Proving ready sources of justification for ever stronger leadership, war and technological expertise have increased this symbolic distance. No crisis like an international one sends politicians, journalists, and academicians scurrying for more rationalizations for increased power, particularly centralized power. And in the name of national unity for waging international war, domestic participation can be drastically reduced, by force if necessary.

REPRESENTATIVE GOVERNMENT IN TRANSITION: TOWARD MORE STRINGENT OLIGARCHIES

Even a more realistic view of elections and participation appears highly utopian in today's world of expanding oligarchic power. Typically, electoral politics is criticized and often destroyed in the name of rigid, hierarchical efficiency, for competitive voting, no matter how ritualized, can be disruptive and inefficient. Efficiency has become the bench mark for today's governments, and with this efficiency, the ancillary value of disciplined, organizational rationality has grown important. In the name of "development" or "modernization" urgent priorities such as national unity are established, which contribute enormously to the politics of power. Citizens turn their backs on representative democracy, for which they have little or no aptitude, and swear allegiance to more efficient forms of power. If power is the only alternative, as citizens are conditioned to believe, then why should they not institute power that works? Again, few stop to ask if the trouble is not with power per se, whether weak or strong, and if the remedy is not a more novel form of politics, one that places greater emphasis on the kind of participation and education that liberates citizens. Does the new power politics really work any better? People in the nearly universal culture of power become so socialized that they think first in terms of strong leadership; those few with second thoughts are usually too late.

Ostensibly so important a means of participation, voting turns out less impressive on closer inspection. Some might argue, however (as a number of specialists in the politics of developing nations do today), that even without competitive voting, modernization encourages mass participation in power calculations.[13] After all, the great revolutions and independence movements of our time find their directions with mass impetus. Hence Nazism, Communism and Nasserism all provide forms of broadened participation, in as much as they all involve masses of people mobilized for various political purposes. Again, however, participation as viewed here is not an aspect of power, as mass mobilization is, but another side of politics. The idea of "mass participation" is an aspect of the politics of power, because, as de Tocqueville so presciently observed about mass society, the simple fact that millions are shepherded as "equal" participants into plebiscites for despots, by no means adds to civic virtue and true participatory politics. That millions rather than thousands now make "demands" on the "system" by no means mitigates the new oligarchies, for these oligarchies are specially geared to generate and manipulate mass demands (in the more polite language of political science, "to aggregate demands") without feeling the effects of spontaneous participation.[14] Curiously, though the one virtue the "masses" possess is their spontaneity, contemporary mass movements are usually opposed to spontaneity. Here, as in voting, "participation" loses some important potentialities as it joins the politics of power as a "function" of that power. Where these new hierarchies prove inefficient in aggregating demands, so that participants get out of hand in factional disputes, other oligarchic forms await to test their special methods. Three forms of accentuated power, corporatism, bureaucracy, and military organization, will be examined here.

Corporatism

Modern corporatism involves a politics by plural interest groups, no one group a majority.[15] Such government gives substance to John Calhoun's ideal of the "concurrent majority," where various interests must be pulled into a coalition sufficiently numerous to constitute a majority, but in the process the numerical majority is subject to checks by groups affiliated with the majority. American society, with its decidedly pluralistic social and economic structures, best fits this ideal. Surely it can be argued that if traditional representative forms no longer fulfill the political needs of contemporary societies, this newer form of representation, the political interest group, can do a much better job for the democratic model. Particularly between elections, as elected leaders sink out of sight into the recesses of complex government, our favorite interests have "representatives" on the scene to watch matters. Through these groups both representation and an opportunity to participate indirectly in making public policy occur. Though the sum total of interests will never equal an aggregate Humpty Dumpty called "public interest," at least most will "get in their licks at the public salt block." Even during elections, when many are confused by the shiny tinsel of Madison Avenue candidate images, the more wordly-wise political minorities see that their interests are well cared for within the party panoply. In other words, with the decline of traditional, popularly elected institutions and the waning of the truly crucial vote has come a rise in interest group power, so that both representation and democracy now fit only into a corporative context. The actual formal institutions are less important than the corporative reality—the "group pressures"—which breathe life into these institutions.

Behind the textbook image of the interest group as tribune of the people lurk some nagging questions, however. If one defines interest groups roughly along the guidelines posted by David B. Truman of Columbia University, as groups of persons with shared attitudes making claims on other groups for establishing and enhancing their aims, and then if one adds that when such groups organize for political action, they are called "political interest groups," one sees immediately that these groups belong to the politics of power.[16] Where claims on other groups are established with the object of enhancing a special group's aims, conflict erupts. In order to operate effectively in this context, these groups, like national states bent on aggrandizement within an international arena of rivalry and war, must organize themselves to fight power with power. Thus groups "mobilize" for political action and "struggle" with each other, much like armies going to war.

Such mobilization takes the form of a power structure within the interest group. Here, as with representation of all kinds, leaders are empowered to act jointly, in advance, on behalf of their constituents and to bind them by their collective decisions. In other words, the same principle of *plena potestas* operates within the broader public context of power and in the narrower confines of special interests. But interestingly enough, while traditional parliamentary institutions evolved into more democratized forms by adding the principle of open, free, and competitive elections, with ample opportunity given the opposition both before and after decisions are made, this same evolution toward democratization has not occurred in most private corporative groups in the United States. As a result, the great organizations of labor, business, medicine, and even science, resemble more the medieval versions of representative government by notables than they do the democratized versions found in nineteenth- and twentieth-century Europe and America. At the peak of American political interests invariably stand oligarchies who specialize in controlling organized groups, but with little or no orderly responsibility to their followers. In many instances, the great "lords temporal," as Adolf A. Berle, Jr. calls them, heading giant corporations, trade associations, and the like, are about as responsible to the rank-and-file members in their organizations (the ordinary citizens in their capacities as group members) as fourteenth-century English parliamentarians were to "the poorest he" in England.[17] Few private interest groups organized for political action in America could be called "democratic" in any sense of the word, after their internal organization is examined. No wonder an American student of science and government, Don K. Price, has recently resorted to feudalistic terminology in describing the "four estates"—scientific, professional, administrative, and political—that dominate American private and public governments.[18]

How then, within a modern context, can these groups be thought to represent the interests of sizeable minorities who voluntarily join or are forced to join their ranks? How are members' demands articulated from bottom to top? The answer to these questions is usually that there is no route organized for such articulation, since there exist no periodic elections for a standing legislative body, no competing parties within the organizations, and no system of adjudicating claims; in other words, rank-and-file membership seldom if ever has a chance to participate. Instead, the theory of "virtual representation," so attractive to the oligarchic, medievalist tastes of that intrepid eighteenth-century conservative, Edmund Burke, fills the gap left by the absence of democratic procedures to make representatives accountable to their constituents. Burke argued, in his famous speech at Bristol, that much as he appreciated his constitutents' concern about his actions in Parliament, he would do as he pleased since he best knew their interests. Though the speech was aimed at an electorate, Burke lived in an era antedating reformed electoral constituencies (which occurred after 1832) and substantially widened suffrage (which occurred after 1867) in England, and a truly popular constituency could never answer him back. Virtual representation, as a theory of representative government, has only a partial bearing on public politics today, both in England and the United States, where representatives have greater leeway depending on a number of factors, although they can never defy their constituents when the latter prove adamant. But in the interest group arena there are many followers of Burke's theory of representation.

The pluralistic euphoria that surrounds minority "representation" through political interest groups, given the increasingly diluted nature of the popular vote for public representatives, seems misguided. Between the ordinary citizen and participation in public policy now stand not only the official elected representatives (so disliked by Rousseau for their adverse effects on popular participation) but also representatives who have no electoral tie whatsoever to common citizens, yet presume to represent the citizens' interests. In the United States, public power has now been supplemented, if not supplanted, by centers of private power even more oligarchic than regular government.[19] The weak citizen, steadily stripped of what little participatory capacity he still has in public politics, now faces irresponsible centers of power in his private world which are even more inimical to his civic virtue. For these private areas of power not only discourage participation but by maintaining the fiction that they are "voluntary," invite any person adopting an independent view relating to their politics to leave the group's premises.[20] Actually, violence (figurative, if not literal) can be exacted against a recalcitrant should he stand on his "rights," because he has no rights under the circumstances of private oligarchy. Furthermore, in some instances the group is really involuntary for all practical purposes (as in county medical societies and some trade unions), so the invitation to leave is seldom accepted, for its acceptance could mean loss of livelihood or status. Instead, acquiescence and apathy become the normal responses, and in the manner of our closed communications system in Chapter 3, power and acceptance of power reinforce each other. Anyone who has belonged to private interest groups, such as labor unions in the United States, will recall how poor rank-and-file participation is in these groups at every policy-making level; dull "business meetings" at the grass roots and excitement upstairs.

Bureaucracy

Even more prevalent than corporative oligarchies has been the spread of bureaucracy. As so frequently happens in the modern social sciences, a compact delineation of the subject is available in the form of a theory, this one developed by Max Weber.[21] Yet Weber's antiseptic treatment of the subject still reveals bureaucracy's involvement in the politics of power. Indeed, with efficient bureaucratic direction, modern power politics becomes virtually irresistible. And much of the almost total ascendancy of power over participation can be traced to the mutually reinforcing tendencies of historical factors and trends within bureaucracy itself.

Historically, Weber noted a general tendency toward bureaucracy wherever technological advances, urbanization, industrialization, and capitalism have developed concurrently. Since these four features summarize the modern world, it is evident that bureaucracy is here to stay. Such developments have complicated social life as never before, causing ordinary citizens to find ever more efficient ways to utilize limited physical and mental resources. In short, citizens are confronted by a deliberate design for intricate hierarchy. Caught in this hierarchical web, only one response seems practicable, more of the same experience.

As a type of authority—and Weber was thinking of general social organization as one form of control between leaders and led which places bureaucracy in the mainstream of power politics—bureaucracy involves at least six unique features which distinguish it from both traditional forms of authority, relying on hoary sanctions, and from more creative authoritative systems hinging on the personal ability of leaders to muster the necessary legitimacy to sustain themselves ("charismatic" authority). First, bureaucracy has a permanent authority with fixed jurisdictions ordered by rules. Second, bureaucratic organization comprises a firmly ordered system of superiority and subordination. Third, use of written official records for office management is standard procedure. Fourth, expert training for officials is the rule. Fifth, these officials find bureaucratic activity a full-time job, a career. And sixth, the management of offices follows general rules.

Aside from the fact that bureaucracy is one form of authority, which automatically places it within the politics of power, bureaucracy constitutes fundamentally the exercise of control on the basis of disciplined, organized knowledge or expertise. Such discipline makes bureaucracy oligarchic. Fixed jurisdictions guided by rules represent a compartmentalization antithetical to participation by ordinary citizens. Such compartmentalization also produces a language or jargon with special meanings to bureaucrats as well as offering symbolic gratifications to their clienteles. A firmly ordered system of superiority and subordination increases symbolic distance. Use of written official records creates legions of filing cabinets, many of them locked, in which are records accessible in most cases only to select employees. Expert training pulls leaders and citizens farther apart, with the experts having special "secrets" of their trade which no citizen can master unless he is socialized within the system. Gone is the "happy versatility" that Pericles celebrated in his oration on the Athenian participatory political system. Having many officials with careers further differentiates government and citizens by setting up a bureaucratic profession with its own interests; again, Rousseau's fears about representative institutions come very much alive, though bureaucracy is representative only in that it reflects social reality, and not in necessarily being accountable to society. And the management of offices by standardized operating procedures creates an environment that disciplines participants and wards off outsiders.

Modern government has become, to a large extent, bureaucratic government. This applies to the governments of both national states and private interests.[22] The tendencies of bureaucracy are even more plainly oligarchic, in the sense of rigidly separating leaders and led and providing little accountability by bureaucrats to their constituents, than are the key aspects of interest group power. Again, however, bureaucracy has proved highly instrumental in the growth of private and public centers of power. Constant argument has developed, as in the case of British nationalized industries, about the "accountability" of these giant bureaucracies both to ordinary citizens and more traditional parliamentary procedures. It is a tribute to the participatory tradition in British politics that this debate continues, but it is also indicative of the impotency of participation in the face of the new oligarchies of interest and bureaucracy that little or nothing is done to create such accountability. The ordinary member of Parliament in England, whose House of Commons stands at the bottom of the list of power institutions in the United Kingdom, can do very little, except by occasionally addressing an acerbic question to a Cabinet minister—who usually avoids any detailed responsibility for a corporation like the British Coal Board. Furthermore, the minister is bound both by law and by the ethic of more efficient administration not to mix the politics of participation with bureaucracy's power. Since Parliament has passed the legal restrictions on what ministers can do, it has only itself to blame, but Parliament is in the grips of disciplined party leadership and has no choice but to pass such legislation.

The principle of some kind of central accounting office, such as the Swedish *Ombudsman* (now to be tried in Great Britain as well), where grievances against the bureaucracy can be checked out by an independent government official and his staff, holds some promise for better accountability, if not actual participation by citizens in administrative activities.[23]

Today an "organization universe" is taken for granted, as self-evident as those "truths" in the American Declaration of Independence were to Jefferson. According to a leading contemporary systems theorist, Anatol Rapoport, even political science has become a science of organization that will advance when general organization theory advances.[24]

Military Organization

The spread of interest oligarchies and bureaucracy, together with the corresponding erosion of traditional representative democracy, constitutes the normal pattern for states like England and the United States where older democratic forms have a long tradition but are now simply being worn away by changing political cultures. These cultures have always emphasized some form of power, but now the emphasis has become exaggerated.

Where representative democracy has never had firm footing, the transition from democracy to oligarchy is apt to be more dramatic, more punctuated with violent contrasts. The true antithesis to the politics of participation is war, with its values and organizational forms starkly opposed to participatory arrangements. War's prime agents are military officials. Surely war has much to do with changing political culture, even in traditional democracies. But where democracy has proved weak or nonexistent, the new form of oligarchy likely to supplant the old often appears as an actual military group or military-type organization, for in this case no tradition of participation exists to counter the most blatant of modern oligarchic forms.

The outstanding form of modern oligarchy has been totalitarianism. This is not the place to list the various characteristics certain authors have ascribed to totalitarian government, but one salient feature of totalitarian organization is interesting for our purposes, its parallels to military order. Hitler frankly patterned his Nazi state after a military command with military ranks.[25]

While the Communist Party under Lenin and Stalin used civilian titles for party positions, both early Communist leaders expressed considerable interest in military organization. Lenin was fascinated with the subject as he envisaged Bolshevik cadres in conspiracy against the old Russian Empire before 1917. After the Bolshevik victory Lenin continued to employ military imagery, such as figures of speech dealing with "machine-gunning" those who might "retreat" from party battles against capitalism. Stalin, in his *Problems of Leninism* (1934) frankly referred to the Communist Party as the "General Staff of the proletariat."[26]

In both Nazi and Soviet cases the animosity against participatory politics with its allegiance to the values of subjective freedom and cosmopolitan humanism has been startling.[27] Nowhere else has there been such systematic "cleansing" from the body politic of cosmopolitanism, subjectivity, peaceful goodwill to all on domestic and foreign planes, and intellectual uniqueness. In direct violation of the ideal of social peace, systematic terror has been liberally employed, through ideological and physical means, against "deviant" classes, private individuals, and public officials. Hence the most dramatic contrast to citizen participation was needed for the most violent assault on participatory politics: The answer was an absolutely disciplined military camp as the proper model for political organization.

Elsewhere, military leaders have actually come to power, sometimes developing elaborate authoritarian organizations complete with bureaucratic and even totalitarian methods, in the process changing from outright military government to an authoritarian civilian model, and at other times employing regular military forces as means of governance. This situation has occurred often in the developing nations of Africa, Asia, Latin America, and the Middle East, where representative democracy has failed to find congenial soil within political cultures very different from those in Western Europe and the United States. Besides, representative institutions are declining in importance within the cradle of their birth, so why should they be expected to succeed elsewhere? The transition to outright military oligarchy has also taken place where independence movements, dedicated to a manipulated shadow of true participatory politics, have failed to cope with the three almost insurmountable crises they face upon gaining their goal of independent nationhood: political disunity, social backwardness, and economic underdevelopment.

Whether it is the artificial military organizations of totalitarian states or direct military rule in the developing nations, the fact remains that military organization, as a form of the politics of power, is here to stay. Along with corporatism and bureaucracy, military organization completes the triumvirate of accentuated forms of power politics, all in contrast to traditional representative institutions, all more deeply antagonistic to the politics of participation. All three of these new power forms have proved extremely capable of perpetuating themselves and spawning numerous progeny. All have mobilized mass support by "engineering consent" instead of "the consent of the governed," an engineering feat even more successfully accomplished with the assistance of modern technology.

This chapter has been concerned primarily with the logic of power and only in a secondary way with the empirical causes for the decay of representative institutions into more stringent oligarchical forms. Surely a foremost cause of this decay, assuming the causes for advancing oligarchy to be multiple, is the state of rapidly advancing technology in modern industrialized nations. This technology has been most astonishing in the areas of communications, transportation, and warfare, and the power of government in relation to ordinary citizens has increased enormously upon the incorporation of this technology into the art and science of governing advanced states. For example, totalitarianism would be inconceivable as a form of government without these technological potentials (though these alone do not explain totalitarianism), and since these possibilities are twentieth-century developments, this makes totalitarianism, (for this among other reasons), a new form of government.[28]

On the other hand, while technological advances surely help to explain the new stringency of power discussed in this chapter, they by no means explain everything. The logic of power has, one could argue, its own inner, historical dynamism which tends to be antithetical to participation and participatory values, whatever the current technology. Given the proper means and convenient excuses—excuses chiefly connected with continuous warfare which is itself the product of power politics—the politics of power will whittle away at participation, even in ostensibly "democratic" systems, and even in technologically underdeveloped nations. Technological advances might just as easily be used in the cause of participation in an effort to decrease political distances between citizens, and so forth. But instead these advances are used against participation, for those in power can enlist the latest techniques for their own efforts since they control the authoritative allocation of resources or at least have an excellent opportunity to control these resources.

Notes to Chapter 4

1. On participatory values in the United States, see Gabriel Almond and Sidney Verba, *The Civic Culture* Princeton, N.J.: (Princeton University Press, 1963), pp. 440 455.

2. The UNESCO survey on democracy is recorded and discussed at length in Richard McKeon, ed., *Democracy in a World of Tensions*, (Chicago: University of Chicago Press, 1951). The general concern of this chapter for modern democracy's dilemmas in the politics of power has been confronted at length by David Spitz in his *Democracy and the Challenge of Power* (New York: Columbia University Press, 1958).

3. See the voluminous record compiled by the Michigan Survey Research Center and various public opinion organizations concerning levels of civic knowledge in the United States. For two assessments of this material by a leading political scientist, the latter book published posthumously as a defense of the "rationality" of the American electorate in presidential elections, see V. O. Key, *Public Opinion and American Democracy* (New York: Alfred A. Knopf, 1961); and *The Responsible Electorate*, with the assistance of Milton C. Cummings (Cambridge, Mass.: Harvard University Press, 1966). The relationship between behavioral science and the increasing tendency of everyone to view politics as something "habitual," is argued by Hannah Arendt in *The Human Conditions* (New York: Doubleday & Company, Inc., 1958), pp. 294–295. The economist Anthony Downs, however, insists that the voter is acting rationally by taking shortcuts, but Downs's model for rationality is the individual consumer who maximizes his utilities. There appears some contradiction in Downs's formulation, since shortcuts may hide valuable information necessary for some political choices. See Anthony Downs, *An Economic Theory of Democracy* (New York: Harper and Row, Publishers, 1957), pp. 37–38.

4. Most work on political participation in the field of political science deals with how nonleaders relate to leaders, and in particular with the subject of voting. For example, see Lester Milbrath, *Political Participation* (Stokie, Ill.: Rand McNally & Company 1965), Figure 3, "Hierarchy of Political Involvement," p. 18.

5. On "activists," see V. O. Key, *Public Opinion and American Democracy*, pp. 536–543.

6. The relationships between bureaucratic managers and legislators were discussed by John Stuart Mill as early as 1861 in *Representative Government*, chapters 5 and 6. Given the British parliamentary tradition, Mill's tone was optimistic concerning the future of creative politics as contrasted with the growing bureaucratic routine of modern life. His tone may also have been a function of the period in which he wrote. In contrast to this optimism, see Max Weber's concern about the future of the "passion and perspective" of politics in the bureaucratic state, in "Politics as a Vocation" (1918), in *From Max Weber: Essays in Sociology* ed. by Hans Gerth and C. Wright Mills, (New York: Oxford University Press), 1958, pp. 77–128.

7. See the discussion of role styles among American state legislators in John C. Wahlke and others, *The Legislative System* (New York: John Wiley & Sons, Inc., 1962), Part 4.

8. The tremendous symbolic distance between the American poor and the centers of American power has been vividly pictured by Michael Harrington, *The Other America* (New York: Crowell-Collier and Macmillan, Inc., 1962), chapter 1. Defining politics as power, Max Weber argued that the politician must let "realities work upon him with inner concentration and calmness." To these ends of concentration and calmness, the politician needs to keep his "distance" from things and men. See Weber, "Politics as a Vocation," p. 115. What can be more distant than the personages, events, and organizations described in high school government textbooks, or the ubiquitous pictures of George Washington in school rooms?

9. One student of Freud has suggested that Life and Death may be antithetical *only* under conditions of social repression very much like what is called "the politics of power" in this essay. It is possible to conceive of social conditions where such an antithesis would not prevail. See Norman O. Brown, *Life against Death* (New York: Alfred A. Knopf, 1959), pp. 106–107. In this sense, the "care" (*Sorge*) for death in the writings of Martin Heidegger appeals to some contemporary social philosophers, but the ethical implications of this "care" are very unclear. For Heidegger's possible relevance to political analysis and political ethics, see Robert J. Pranger, *Action, Symbolism, and Order, the Existential Dimensions of Politics in Modern Citizenship* (Nashville, Tenn.: Vanderbilt University Press, 1968), chapters III-IV, VI.

10. Ernst Cassirer argued that to understand the "perceptual space" within which we act as human beings, we must understand "symbolic space," for man is by nature *animal symbolicum*. Further, symbolization means representation, and representation involves deliberate use of reason, as contrasted with primitive habit. Clearly, politics loses its richness as a humanizing venture when it is reduced to sheer habitual response. On the question of symbolic space, see Cassirer, *An Essay on Man* (New York: Doubleday & Company, Inc., 1944), pp. 62–79. On "space" in politics, see Sheldon S. Wolin, *Politics and Vision* (Boston:

Little, Brown & Company, 1960), p. 7; and Hannah Arendt, *The Human Condition*, chapter 2.

11. Robert Boguslaw, an expert on computer systems, reports that even "key decision makers" are increasingly seen, by some organizations, as hangers-on. All too frequently the question today becomes "but the program can't handle it," meaning that the "design" of the "system" will not allow for deviation from a previously established code. See Robert Boguslaw, *The New Utopians* (Englewood Cliffs, N. J.: Prentice-Hall, Inc., 1965), p. 185.

12. See Stanley Kelley, Jr., *Public Relations and Political Power* (Baltimore: The Johns Hopkins Press, 1956); and Joseph A. Schumpeter, *Capitalism, Socialism and Democracy*, 3d ed. (New York: Harper and Row, Publishers, 1950), Part 4, chapters 21-23.

13. For example, the argument of Ruth Schachter, "Single-Party Systems in West Africa," in Harry Eckstein and David E. Apter, eds., *Comparative Politics, A Reader* (New York: The Free Press, 1963), pp. 693-705, especially 702-704. See also Douglas Ashford, *National Development and Local Reform: Political Participation in Morocco, Tunisia and Pakistan* (Princeton, N. J.: Princeton University Press, 1967) for a similar discussion of managed participation.

14. The idea of "aggregating demands" is found under the rubrics of "interest aggregation" and "converting demands" in Gabriel Almond and A. Bingham Powell, Jr., *Comparative Politics, A Developmental Approach* (Boston: Little, Brown & Company, 1966), chapter 5. The authors discuss "controlled participation" (p. 113).

15. On advancing corporatism as it affects political practices in two modern societies, see Grant McConnell, *Private Power and American Democracy* (New York: Alfred A. Knopf, 1966); and Samuel H. Beer, *British Politics in the Collectivist Age* (New York: Alfred A. Knopf, 1965).

16. For his complete definition of "political interest group," see David B. Truman, *The Governmental Process* (New York: Alfred A. Knopf, 1951), p. 33.

17. On the modern corporate "lords temporal" and the need for a new "lords spiritual," see Adolf A. Berle, Jr., *Economic Power and the Free Society* (New York: Fund for the Republic, 1957); and *The 20th Century Capitalist Revolution* (New York: Harcourt, Brace & World, Inc., 1954), chapter 5.

18. His analysis of the "four estates" may be found in Don K. Price, *The Scientific Estate* (Cambridge, Mass.: Harvard University Press, 1965), pp. 132-136. However, Price sees science as a liberalizing estate.

19. Seymour Martin Lipset and his associates cite the International Typographical Union (ITU) as an exception to the oligarchic tendencies of organizations. But at the end of their study, they warn that this exception may very well prove the rule instead of contradicting it, given the herculean efforts necessary to protect against oligarchy. See Seymour Martin Lipset, *Union Democracy* (Garden City, N. Y.: Doubleday & Company, Inc., 1962), pp. 452ff.

20. On the "voluntary" aspects of "private government," see McConnell, Part 1, chapter 5.

21. For Weber's theory of "legal authority" with employment of a "bureaucratic administrative staff," see Max Weber, *The Theory of Social and Economic Organization*, trans. by A. M. Henderson and Talcott Parsons, ed. by T. Parsons (New York: The Free Press, 1947), pp. 333-341.

22. The ubiquity of "bureaucracy" is more and more commented upon in terms of an "age of organization." In spite of some views that modern organiza-

tions are more pluralistic than folk wisdom would believe, the fact remains that on the crucial question of basic policies and sanctions, organizations tend to be quite centralized, even while allowing operational decisions a certain latitude. Also, pluralistic and democratic bureaucracies are never synonymous organizations. See Raul Hilberg's massive treatment of pluralism among Nazi bureaucracies, *The Destruction of the European Jews* (Chicago: Quadrangle Books, 1961, 1966).

23. On the role of institutionalized critics of bureaucracy, see two books by Walter Gellhorn, *Ombudsmen and Others, Citizen's Protectors in Nine Countries* (Cambridge, Mass.: Harvard University Press, 1966); and *When Americans Complain, Governmental Grievance Procedures* (Cambridge, Mass.: Harvard University Press, 1966). Gellhorn tends to minimize the growth of bureaucracy, since "good" nations do institute various controls. On the other hand, both books unconsciously portray the great distances that separate citizens from governments, even in small states such as Sweden. Further, the citizen is always confronting political situations, but he has no role in them; hence, he must employ outside "critics" to speak in his place, just as an "audience" at a play is represented by critics. Meanwhile, the authorized, popularly elected representatives are now two steps removed from the public they serve, with seemingly no power over bureaucracies at all. Nonelected bureaucrats who are *not* responsible to elected officials, are the citizens' protectors! In other words, the institution of the *Ombudsmen* raises some fundamental issues about the future role of representative democracy in the contemporary politics of power. With decisions made and controls effected through nonelected officials, citizens are bound to wonder what elected representatives are good for.

24. Rapoport's view is found in "Some System Approaches to Political Theory," in David Easton, ed., *Varieties of Political Theory* (Englewood Cliffs, N. J.: Prentice-Hall, Inc., 1966), at 140–141. For some critical remarks about the conversion of politics into organization, see Wolin, chapter 10.

25. Hitler's interest in military organization is best seen in Alan Bullock, *Hitler, A Study in Tyranny*, rev. ed. (New York: Harper and Row, Publishers, 1964), p. 403, and elsewhere. For a different position on this subject, both insisting on the *militaristic* position of Hitler and his inner elite, but at the same time arguing that the Nazi movement was not primarily *military* in organization, see Hannah Arendt, *The Origins of Totalitarianism* 2d ed. (New York: Meridian Books, Inc., 1958), pp. 369–371. Totalitarianism has received such extensive treatment that it does not seem necessary to go into particulars here. Also, it is now evident that totalitarianism is a much more unique—and perhaps brutally transient—extension of power than the more common oligarchic developments discussed here.

26. Lenin's statement, "When a real army is in retreat, machine guns are set up. . . ." can be found in full in Merle Fainsod, *How Russia Is Ruled* (Cambridge, Mass.: Harvard University Press, 1951), p. 137.

27. Hannah Arendt discusses totalitarianism's animosity toward these values in *The Origins of Totalitarianism*, chapter 13.

28. See Hans J. Morgenthau, "Modern Science and Political Power," *Columbia Law Review*, 64 (December 1964), 1386–1409; Jacques Ellul, *The Technological Society*, trans. by John Wilkinson (New York: Alfred A. Knopf, 1964); Philip Green, "Science, Government, and the Case of RAND, A Singular Pluralism" (review article), *World Politics*, XX (January 1968), 301–326. Green's

review also provides additional bibliographic information about the idea of pluralism in contemporary political science and also about criticisms that have been levelled against the pluralist position.

Chapter 5

THE BETTER THE CONSTITUTION OF A STATE
IS, THE MORE DO PUBLIC AFFAIRS ENCROACH
ON PRIVATE IN THE MINDS OF THE
CITIZENS. . . . IN A WELL-ORDERED CITY
EVERY MAN FLIES TO THE ASSEMBLIES;
UNDER A BAD GOVERNMENT NO ONE CARES
TO STIR A STEP TO GET TO THEM, BECAUSE
NO ONE IS INTERESTED IN WHAT HAPPENS
THERE, BECAUSE IT IS FORESEEN THAT THE
GENERAL WILL NOT PREVAIL, AND LASTLY
BECAUSE DOMESTIC CARES ARE ALL-AB-
SORBING . . . . AS SOON AS ANY MAN SAYS OF
THE AFFAIRS OF THE STATE, "WHAT DOES IT
MATTER TO ME?" THE STATE MAY BE GIVEN
UP FOR LOST.

Rousseau
The Social Contract

. . . POLITICS IS NOT LIKE THE NURSERY; IN
POLITICS OBEDIENCE AND SUPPORT ARE THE
SAME.

Hannah Arendt
Eichmann in Jerusalem

5

Citizenship as Participation

This chapter will deal with citizenship as participation, a phrase which implies that the citizen's primary role is to create a politics, not to function as an appendage, or mere participant, for the structure of power. Here it is significant that the Greek term for citizen, *politēs*, comes from the same root as "politics" and means he who collaborates openly or publicly in making a common union. To lose the citizen, therefore, means to lose some valuable aspects of politics; or perhaps the citizen's demise represents the decline of certain fundamental concomitants of political life, notably personal freedom, public action, and common involvement. Yet it is through the citizen's activities that these concomitants are sustained, and so the decline of citizenship and the evaporation of these fundamentals reciprocally affect each other in a vicious circle.

It has been argued thus far that the basic role the citizen plays involves participating in a common union to meet and to resolve differences with a minimum of violence. Participation helps create this common union. The formation process goes on incessantly. As the process continues, individuals define themselves as human beings, brought by their participation into wider views about self and others. In other words, citizens discover themselves as *civil*-ized human beings through this type of politics. With others, they uncover the potentialities implicit in their humanity, but these potentialities never exhaust themselves ín the actuality of any moment. Thus it is particularly important that objective knowledge about what "is" or "has been" should not dominate political education. But such objectivity depends upon the prevailing political culture, as noted earlier in Chapter 3.

The inquiry after human potential is ceaseless, open-ended, and subject to trial and error. The politics of participation offers one important avenue for conducting this search, because it emphasizes those methods, values, and actions that widen human horizons.

This chapter will deal with the political culture of participation. First, the political objects found in participatory politics, the actors, actions, and settings for this culture, will be examined. Then the subjective political culture of participation will be discussed, including a summary of the values promoted by participation.

THE OBJECTS
IN THE CULTURE OF PARTICIPATORY POLITICS

To counter the utopian ideal of a politics without power, where civic virtue runs the state and leadership becomes subordinate, the myth of universal power has arisen. In the name of realism it is held that power and the attendant evils of power lie at the heart of all politics. This may be true for the politics of power but not for all politics.

Politics and the *politēs* are indissoluably linked, and the citizen's chief responsibility is participating, not pursuing power, hence all politics is *not* power. To destroy the citizen, in turn, one first eliminates his *raison d'être*; but such destruction limits politics severely. Thus, realism has concentrated on what cannot be denied in contemporary politics, the ubiquity of power, but has neglected what should not be forgotten, the potentialities of politics. In the end the realism of power becomes the most illusory of myths, for while it dulls the appetite for political potentials, it seeks solutions to the harmful evils promoted by power, such as international conflict, with the means of power. If only the world's elites could understand each other's interests, goes one argument, then they might communicate for peace. But these leaders understand each other only too well; they all speak the competitive language of power. Or perhaps just one more summit conference between the USSR and the United States, preceded by skillful secret diplomacy at lower levels, might solve things. But who will attend such meetings? Only the representatives of power are eligible, and thus a closed circle develops.

Political power promotes the distinctive values of power. Unless some view of politics can be established that divorces at least some political activity from power, a political culture becomes lopsided and human potential is short-circuited. This does not mean that politics ought to be done away with, but only that its potentials for civilizing should be maximized. To live in a civil society is the first step toward civilization; such a society comes about only through political activity. Yet the most dangerous of all political myths is not the one that seeks to divorce politics from power, but the one that encourages citizens to believe that somehow power will cure its own harmful effects: The question, therefore, is not one of eradicating power, for this is idle dreaming, but of mitigating the extreme consequences of power by introducing another political form, participation. It resolves into a question of developing a situation where the two forms of politics, power and participation, work together without either consuming the other.

Earlier, the objects of political culture in the politics of power were surveyed (Chapter 2). There was also a brief discussion of the major features present in the politics of participation (Chapter 3). This chapter will cover more thoroughly the unique objects and the political vocabulary linked to such features found in the culture of participatory politics. These unique objects include (*a*) citizens as "participators" (actors) in forming a common union, (*b*) their "horizontal relationships" (actions), and (*c*) "circumferences," or levels of participation (settings). ("Object" refers to a salient feature, *not* to a real person—see Chapter 2.)

Citizens as Participators

The first object in the politics of participation is the central civic position, the participator, a vital decision-making role readily open to all members. "To participate" means "to join in," as one might join in singing a song. For citizenship, the major issue concerns the quality of this participation. Joining something may mean one of two things, either attaching oneself to an on-going process and then performing certain specified functions in that process as a "participant," or else contributing something unique to the process one joins, thus becoming a "participator" in that process. The distinction between participant and participator was alluded to earlier when it was noted that the best one can say for citizens in the politics of power is that they are participants who orient themselves upward toward their government, that area where real decisionmakers, the powerful leaders, hold sway.[1] One can make the distinction clearer by using Arthur Koestler's dividing line between creative and routine operations in science: Creativity involves "bisociative" leaps from one area to another through analogies, while normal science is "associative" in the sense that it operates in well-worn paths as constant emendation.[2] The politics of participation encourages the citizen as a participator, a creative contributor to politics; the politics of power discourages all but a few in this creativity ("leadership"), stimulating instead associative activity among citizens ("followership"). This appears even in standard political vocabulary, for when one speaks of the politics of power in political science one uses expressions like "function," "socialization," "response," and even "prediction." A politics of participation would need, perhaps, a different language, one placing more emphasis on unpredictability, education, and so forth.[3]

In other words, the politics of participation emphasizes mass creativity. Actually, the number of citizens involved as participators will vary with the occasion. But this much seems certain: In participatory politics the focus is on the citizenry, not on leadership. Such a politics may be inimical to order, for sobriety is not necessarily a cardinal citizen virtue, whatever its benefits for a stable society. Bisociative leaps in the history of science are connected with scientific revolutions: Likewise in politics, civic creativity may lead to crises and revolutions.[4] But such conflict will not resemble the clash of mighty nations with their vast reserves of mobilized citizens, nor will it resemble those revolutions, such as Russia's in 1917, captivated by appeals and directions from party elites.

A paradox arises here, however: Only through creative political experiences can a society discover the best political action in the politics of participation. Yet citizens, more used to the politics of power, are mostly unfit to engage themselves in such new experiences with any expertise; disabled by their political culture, they prove uninterested and ignorant. Thus political participation may destroy itself either by lapsing nostalgically into order and authority (the tested way of doing things) or by succumbing to its own excesses (mass energies can lead to authoritarian and even totalitarian consequences). Revolutions since 1789 have most often ended in despotism, not freedom.[5]

When one approaches the citizen as participator, one looks at politics from the citizen's viewpoint. He can always look vertically to hierarchy, as earlier noted, thus becoming a participant in the politics of power. But he has the option as well of looking laterally or horizontally to his fellow citizens; this too constitutes a political point of view, though not the viewpoint of power. In the politics of participation the citizen looks to other citizens, not to the powerful. He "orients" himself spatially with horizontal, nonhierarchical referents. Here citizenship becomes a kind of group dynamics involving friends and equals, a spontaneous "field" of the *politēs* where collaborators create a common union. Such collaboration constitutes the substance of participatory action, the second object that demands attention in the political culture of participation.

Participatory Action

What comprises the kind of action undertaken by these civic participators? Imagine eight persons sitting down in a living room to discuss a problem common to their neighborhood, the need for better sewer facilities. At first, idle conversation takes place, establishing some kind of *rapport* among those present, with certain rudimentary social relations already at work based on factors outside the meeting (relative social positions and so on) and on factors inside this *ad hoc* group (conversational ability, an interesting story, and the like). Then small talk ends, and someone opens the more serious questions for discussion and debate. Differing points of view are heard, some perhaps so diverse that unless consensus is reached, the group may end its meeting indecisively or even chaotically. These points of view represent competing claims for the group's common attention; hence, one may speak of the group having a "common interest." During the discussion leaders may emerge—though they are not a necessary (primitive) condition for the existence of a political group—either formally appointed by the group or informally designated for prominence by the more ordinary workings of the group's sociometry.[6] Those presenting alternative arguments may attempt to control the group's directions by influencing its leadership, or the leadership may try to dominate the group. Again, as with leadership itself, such attempts to control are not necessary conditions for a political group. At some point there may or may not be a definitive decision made concerning the group's final direction, but in any case resolution will depend on what transpires during the group's meeting *between* its members. Resolution hinges on participation. Results may be unpredictable, developing from the interaction of members during the time the group meets. Whatever substance develops so far as discussion, leadership, and decision are concerned, follows from a process unique to that particular group, a process depending upon spontaneous interaction among living people in a special situation at a specific time. The key to everything else that takes place may be found in this horizontal, interactive, participative occasion. The movement together into resolution is accomplished, finally, if accomplished at all, without violence or at least with a minimum of overt force.

What emerges here as "politics," the effort by human beings to organize themselves in common undertakings to meet and to resolve their differences by curtailing open violence, depends upon participation among persons and upon nothing else. Hierarchical leadership may develop as one outcome of this participation, but emergent leadership is not what is typically political about the situation. A participation in common exploration of differences and resolutions constitutes a truly political experience. Some group situations are traditionally political, special places set aside historically and institutionally to accomodate competing claims, disputes, and possible resolutions concerning society's common problems. But any group, as a miniature society, may experience political action at some time, as interactions take place among its members over matters of common concern to that society. Again, it is between people that politics arises, develops, and disappears. All one can say is that some groups are, in this sense, "more political" than others. Suppose that our hypothetical neighborhood group never meets again? Does its evanescence destroy the argument that this group is political? No. A political group experiences some special action between its members. This experience distinguishes such a group from others. Most important, however, it is not the special attributes of a group that make it political, but what goes on inside the group between its members.

Given this view of politics as a special sort of action between full members in a society, and that potential in any and every social group that claims the allegiance of a membership, the tasks of a truly political theory seem herculean. What is the scope for a study of politics based on this type of analysis? The answer to this question is both simple and difficult: simple, because the central focus is between persons; difficult, because such relationships occur continuously, simultaneously, and ubiquitously. In American politics, for instance, it is possible that these relations appear every minute of every day; indeed, this is what a "political process" really involves, a kind of never-ending flow of special events or situations taking place between persons and groups around the block and around the world. To catalogue these events definitively would be impossible, to delimit them to some special area would be arbitrary.

Analytically speaking, the matter of limiting what is political seems fairly easy. Of all the relations between persons and groups of persons, only some are political—those dealing with efforts to organize in common undertakings to meet and resolve differences through curtailed violence. Basically, these relations conform to the model of a neighborhood discussion group given earlier. In such a group there is really no stable "system"; its evanescence makes it impossible to speak of its "persistence," a topic of great interest to what has been called "systems analysis" in contemporary political science (as noted earlier, the vocabulary of systems is appropriate to the politics of power).[7] But is it really a distinguishing mark of political situations that they "persist" over time, or is it just that some such situations, supported by specially organized hierarchies, endure longer than others? Probably the latter answer is more accurate. Any situation among people can be political if there appears a common focus established for a specific problem, if alternative claims relating to that problem appear, and if efforts are made to adjust these claims through adjudication. At all stages, however, in establishing a common interest, in presenting dissident claims, in effecting control, and in adjudicating rivalries, attention shifts from a general system to what goes on among citizens or full members of a group on a given occasion. In politics there exists a narrowing spiral of social involvements from complicated national states, the main consideration here, to neighborhood discussion groups, all connected but growing simpler in their organization as one decreases the circumference of the spiraling loops ("circumference" is explained below). The point is that every loop, no matter how simple its structure, is a political one if one finds the elements of common focus, alternative claims, and adjudication. "Levels" of political activity, as used here, do not parallel exactly "national," "state," and "local" governments but refer to the amount of space and length of chronological time (these two elements going to make up a circumference) various groups occupy within the total political process.

The Circumference of Action

The third type of object found in participatory politics is the circumference of political action defined in terms of participation rather than power. A circumference of political action has to do with how much space—numbers of persons, geographical distance, monetary resources, to name a few variables—and how much chronological time a particular political group occupies.[8] This circumference can also be called a "level" or "setting" for political action (see Chapter 2). An example might help. In one sense, the attributes of political power, all "nations" are equal whether they are the United States or Honduras, because they share certain characteristics. Hence Weber's famous notion of the "political," that agency enjoying a society's legitimate monopoly of the means of force within certain geographical frontiers, would apply equally to the United States and Honduras.[9] But in participatory terms, by judging both nations in terms of relative political circumference, the United States and Honduras are not equal spatially or temporally. On the other hand, General Motors Corporation is, in some respects, more equal politically to Honduras. True, Honduras has an armed force and geographical frontiers—national attributes—while General Motors does not. But General Motors does have a large legal staff and has used, from time to time, public police and hired strikebreakers, to say nothing of its plant police and detective services. In the case of at least one major area of American industry, steel, even the armed power of the United States government has fallen before a large legal staff busy in the federal courts. The frontiers of General Motors, a corporate status, are more securely protected by law against outside aggressors than are Honduras' geographical frontiers, guaranteed under flimsy international law. From the standpoint of numbers of persons involved (if the clientele is included as part of General Motors' overall organization), amount of geographical distance covered by marketing operations, extent of monetary resources, and period of uninterrupted organizational development, General Motors is much more comparable to Honduras than Honduras to the United States.

By the criteria of political actions between people, General Motors has its politics, though it is perhaps not as single-mindedly devoted to politics as either the United States or Honduras. But General Motors is a political enterprise nevertheless; the national state does not monopolize politics. Within this automotive giant's structure one finds common interests or focuses where rival claimants seek control of the group's direction and influence adjudication of claims. Wherever the idea of "group policy" occurs,—in the automobile industry, the struggle between nations, or in a neighborhood association—it can be predicted that politics will arise within a particular group. Policy making, which means the framing of common interests for a group, involves politics, politicians, and citizens, no matter what the group.

What varies from group to group is the extensiveness of political action in terms of space and time, and whether the group has a predominately power- or participation-centered culture. But one could argue that qualitatively it is meaningless to divide "political" from "nonpolitical" in terms of artificial institutions with certain attributes, since this division runs counter to experience and logic. When one says that a group is "politically involved," therefore, one should mean that something about its own interactions have turned political, not that the group has now entered the swirl of public politics.

Even if one allows a wider view of politics, one might fairly ask whether participatory circumferences of action are not confined to small *ad hoc* groups like neighborhood meetings. An example of a wider circumference of action, participatory in nature, has been cited by Jean-Paul Sartre.[10] Describing the French Resistance community during the Second World War, "The Republic of Silence," as a "true democracy," Sartre argued that there existed an "equality of risks" for all involved in battling the Nazis, from message carriers to top leaders, "the same danger, the same destitution, the same total responsibility, the same absolute liberty in discipline." In this solitude, where each relied only on himself, each knew that when he chose freedom for himself, he chose liberty for everyone. Yet this "Republic" was without institutions, army, and police; in other words, it lacked a well-organized hierarchy supported by bureaucracy, a politics of power. Sartre's picture of the Resistance, whatever its empirical accuracy, represents a fine vision of the politics of participation, a politics that accentuates the individual citizen's responsibility for the freedom of all as that citizen makes political decisions for himself, a participative politics that focuses laterally from each member to his confreres, instead of upward toward leadership. This horizontal focus from individual member to fellow citizens constitutes the subjective culture of participative politics, the next topic of this chapter. Such a focus varies with a total cultural context, and not with the single variable of size.

The idea of a "circumference of action" has relevance both for the politics of power and the politics of participation. It has been singled out within the context of participation for a special reason, however. The argument that size and complexity inhibit horizontally organized groups and necessitate strong leadership is born out by neither experience nor logic. Several types of group settings that are conducive for participation might be mentioned which depend more on the "spirit" or culture of the group than on its size. Protest, individual and collective, is a form of participation. Among various types of protest groups are *ad hoc* ones, like the neighborhood association, though both larger and smaller, and action groups where emphasis is on the mutual interactions of members rather than on the achievement of power. *Ad hoc* and action groups may form for other than protest issues also. Then there are informal groupings within formal, hierarchical organizations. Also, deliberate attempts have been made to "flatten" formal hierarchies. Finally, decentralization may encourage civic participation, though no easy equation between decentralization and participatory politics can be made.

THE SUBJECTIVE CULTURE
OF PARTICIPATORY POLITICS

Recall that a four-phased paradigm for subjective political culture was developed in Chapter 3, with phases two, three, and four pertaining to individual responses. Phase one involved an objective culture demanding the citizenry's attention. Phase two concerned political communications links between culture and citizen. Response from the citizen constituted phase three, while the fourth phase dealt with feedback from citizen to culture.

After this review of the objective culture of participation, it is now possible to examine individual responses in the politics of participation within the setting of these objects. Communications in participatory culture tend toward a political education that encourages subjective identity and cosmopolitan awareness. How political participation works to develop such identity and awareness can only be speculated upon, but the following pertinent psychological information offers some clues about this development.

According to Erik H. Erikson, the eight stages of identity transformation in personality and their relation to psychoanalytic maturation levels are: (1) trust vs. basic mistrust (oral sensory level); (2) autonomy vs. shame and doubt (muscular-anal); (3) initiative vs. guilt (locomotor-genital); (4) industry vs. inferiority (latency); (5) identity vs. role diffusion (puberty and adolescence); (6) intimacy vs. isolation (young adulthood); (7) generativity vs. stagnation (adulthood); and (8) integrity vs. disgust, despair (maturity).[11]

In Erikson's judgment some of the above levels appear more crucial than others. Particularly important are the third level, where "the most fateful split and transformation in the emotional powerhouse occurs, a split between potential human glory and potential total destruction,"[12] and the fifth level, where "adolescents have to refight many of the battles of earlier years, even though to do so they must artificially appoint perfectly well-meaning people to play the roles of enemies."[13]

The child's mind, in the locomotor-genital stage (the third level), becomes divided into "an infantile set" which "perpetuates the exuberance of growth potentials" and "a parental set" supporting and increasing "self-observation, self-guidance, and self-punishment."[14] As anyone familiar with Freudian psychology will recognize immediately, the chief problem here is "one of mutual regulation" of id and superego under ego's direction.[15] But it is important to note, for this highlights the importance of the first level as well as the genital problem, more typically Freudian in emphasis, that in adult mental illness traced to the third level, "this direct attack on the organism itself can be attributed to a weakness in underlying trust which makes autonomy bothersome and facilitates a partial regression to the stage of weak homeostasis. . . .the culture had made a man overadvertise himself. . .while he knew all along that his mother never believed in it."[16]

Also vitally important for the growth of personal identity is adolescence (the fifth level), a specialty of Erikson's and of special interest to this study of participation's value for human development. Here all the old battles have to be refought, and then childhood identifications integrated with the individual's endowed aptitudes and his opportunities in society. The final outcome of this renewed conflict and required integration should be an "ego identity," a "new sense of continuity and sameness" that marks off one individual from another.[17] Since the problem in adolescence is to gain an "accrued confidence that the inner sameness and continuity are matched by the sameness and continuity of one's meaning for others, as evidenced in the tangible promise of a 'career,' "[18] the ensuing struggles between ego identity and role diffusion during adolescence hinge upon trust also.

In the context of this adumbration of Erikson's overall scheme, political participation can now be assessed as a vital means for aiding the process of identity transformation in personality. Politics can assist human development here, providing that participatory spaces are expansive enough. My accent is frankly speculative, but plausible in terms of current research on relations between political activity and personality.

Quite clearly Erikson is both retaining the traditional Freudian emphasis on the locomotor-genital stage and insisting that the "basic trust" which develops even earlier through maternal care,[19] and the "ego identity" which comes later in puberty and adolescence, are also vital. Since the question of full-fledged citizenship has traditionally been a question of conscious group commitment at the age of maturity (maturity measured by sexual development and/or age), Erikson's diagnosis of adolescence and young adulthood is very relevant.[20] It should be noted that good citizenship or civic virtue can never rely only on socialization patterns developed in early childhood, and any study of citizenship which concentrates on these patterns to the exclusion of later developments is misleading. The quality of citizenship is measured in terms of the capacity of adults to make sound, conscious, political judgments within adult contexts; this quality can never be learned through childhood citizenship lessons. Thus, citizenship is intrinsically bound up with what Erikson calls "identity formation" in adolescence, which, if successful, produces a person capable of independent judgment and aware of others as autonomous persons in their own right. As will be seen, participation has a great deal to do with both the capacity for independent judgment and the solicitude for other persons as equals.

As far as mature citizenship is concerned, the chief problem areas are adolescence and young adulthood, and the major issue is not the content of political socialization, but the quality of political education. The relevant issue is whether adults will continue to make political judgments as children make them, relying on hierarchical authority with no regard for their own independent decisions. The politics of power tends to encourage such childlike dependence, as noted earlier, but participation does not.

During childhood the family dominates daily life and the child interacts with what Erikson calls a "hierarchy of roles."[21] This is the modal society for the politics of power, prompting some political analysts to locate the state's origins in the family. But personal development is discontinuous, and the self-certainties generated in childhood evaporate as the child grows into an adolescent and then an adult. Adult identity is never simply a sum total of childhood identifications, but requires an ego synthesis to achieve the uniqueness associated with mature adulthood. In this process of discontinuous change from child to adult, the concluding stage of childhood, adolescence, plays a vital role.

Adolescence represents the selective repudiation and absorption of new configurations of childhood identifications, according to Erikson.[22] Without this repudiation and resynthesization, the child will simply not "grow up." Though identity formation is a life-long process, it is during adolescence that role experimentation takes place as the individual faces the problem of identifying himself in the flux of role diffusion; here develops his "identity crisis." In this experimentation and eventual decision to adopt one of many identifying roles, the adolescent needs wider social recognition as much as the child needs maternal care. Such "experimentation" ought to be accomplished in the very best of laboratory situations where destructive, internal conflicts are minimized and thoughtfulness is maximized.

Society, with its objective and subjective culture, provides the laboratories for solving the identity crisis. It is society's responsibility to provide a series of successive environments, more or less discontinuous and yet "culturally and psychologically consistent."[23] This responsibility a society will always face, even when it insists, as in America, that it has no such responsibility. One of the most vital aspects of these laboratories is ideology, or "a utopian simplification of historical perspective" within which the individual may find a "solidarity linking common identities."[24] Erikson's favorite example of "growing up" successfully, within a social situation that provided optimum experimentation while at the same time recognizing this experimentation as valid, is George Bernard Shaw's early membership in the Fabian Society in *fin de siècle* England.

With its loosely structured organization and its emphasis on political education in the sense used here, the Fabian Society conformed well to the idea of a participatory politics. Most important, however, the Fabians were recognized in England as a legitimate, if somewhat eccentric, organization, a place where young men like Shaw could gain the commitment and recognition they needed to establish their identity. The

Fabian Society provided Shaw with both a public outlet for his intellectual brilliance and a "systematically simplified" view of life at a time when he needed both the outlet and the world view. As a form of participatory politics, however, the society did not so dominate the lives of its members that they could never escape it, for according to Erikson the danger with ideology is that after it has helped the ego find identity, it may then demand total, crippling allegiance in return.[25] Such identities, captured by ideologies, are still only in part transformed, since the superego has gained the ascendancy again over the autonomous ego and thus blocked the ego's passage to responsible citizenship. Total world views, which aim to dominate all allegiances, are related to the politics of power in that they are linked to organizations which intend to subordinate all aspects of life to a hierarchy.[26]

The problem in contemporary societies is either no ideology at all, as in America, or ideologies completely dominating the process of ego identity. The American case is, in some respects, as bad as that of a totally ideological society, for where no ideologies exist there remain only mindless stereotypes instead, such as a "business creed." These stereotypes, much like rigid ideologies, are authoritarian in their relentless persecution of dissent. Yet such stereotypes, unlike more rigid ideologies, leave the ego untransformed, since they refuse any explicit, systematic form. Being "in the air," so to speak, stereotypes evade logical analysis and criticism; they confront individuals with no special intellectual challenge but exact only a rigid, unthinking obedience. To question such stereotypes means to revert to negative ideologies pitting the "individual against society," private utopias where each person constitutes a "majority of one."[27]

In the cases of both totalitarian ideologies and stereotyped social creeds, the alternatives for personal development appear to be only two, autocracy or anarchy, the end result in either case being an inevitable violence in both psychological and political terms. There is no space between, only an alienated vacuum, as noted earlier, in which individuals may experiment, but with fear and trembling. The choice with most integrity in this case may be to rebel against "absurd" authority, but it is difficult to say what positive benefits accrue from such an absurdist ethic for either individual or society. In this essay's view, neither state nor citizen can prosper much under these circumstances, whatever the reality of such circumstances and whatever the alleged attractiveness of absurdity for personal life.[28]

Erikson warns about transferring clinical methods to public practice. But he also cautions those in authority not to push young persons into totally negative identities by any ingrown habits of law or psychiatry.[29]

In the case of law, this means—as I see matters—that spaces of "psycho-social moratoria" (Erikson) must be publicly provided, at least in the schools, to insure the development of healthy citizens who, when they reach the age of legal maturity, are also capable of political maturity. Unlike the child, who confronts a hierarchy of roles for which he is not responsible, the adult is a member of such a hierarchy, and sometimes an influential member. His responsibility is that of a full member, not a ward, in those political groups relevant to his life space. Incumbent upon the good member, the virtuous citizen, is the ability to make political decisions which at once protect his own integrity and take cognizance of the integrity of others. But this involves a psychological and political maturity fostered by a society which provides for its neophyte members an adequate *political education* in the form of sufficient participatory experience through ideas and practices consistent with the aims of this education.[30]

American society, as most contemporary societies, fails to provide much spontaneous civic experience, in our case less out of ideological zeal than out of nonideological prejudice. For his political experience the typical American adolescent is confronted by excessive authority in the form of legitimate stereotypes and groups, and by negative, anarchistic, absurdist interactions with his fellows which in turn often metamorphose into highly authoritarian adventures in their own right. The participatory spaces between authority and anarchy are neglected, if not actively dis-criminated against. Authority is promoted, maturity stymied. The adult citizen is almost dead, and with him will vanish the human being, autono-mous and social, we in the Western political tradition have come to respect. What remains is a curiously childlike but hardly exemplary crea-ture, for whom the appropriate human scale is not Shakespeare's Hamlet but Kafka's K.

Notes to Chapter 5

1. The contrasts between "participant" and "participator" can best be seen by examining Lester Milbrath's *Political Participation* (Skokie, Ill.: Rand McNally & Company, 1965), Figure 3, "Hierarchy of Political Involvement," p. 18, and comparing it with this chapter. Milbrath concerns himself exclusively with the "participant", or the way in which the citizen "orients" himself toward power. For a clear statement of the view that participation functions to provide

access to power, see Carl J. Friedrich, *Man and His Government, An Empirical Theory of Politics* (New York: McGraw-Hill, Inc., 1963), pp. 292ff.

2. This distinction is found in Arthur Koestler, *The Act of Creation* (New York: Crowell-Collier and Macmillan, Inc., 1964), Book 2, chapter 10.

3. For two efforts to formulate a vocabulary for political unpredictability or discontinuity, see Hannah Arendt, *The Human Condition* (New York: Doubleday & Company, Inc., 1958), chapter 5; and Dorothy Emmet, *Function, Purpose, and Powers* (London: Macmillan & Co., Ltd., 1958), chapter 6. As Miss Arendt seems to argue, however, experience with political discontinuity depends on the prevailing political culture. See also Robert J. Pranger, *Action, Symbolism, and Order*, chapter IV.

4. On parallels between scientific and political revolutions, see Thomas S. Kuhn, *The Structure of Scientific Revolutions* (Chicago: University of Chicago Press, 1964), pp. 91–93.

5. On revolution and despotism, see Hannah Arendt, *On Revolution* (London: Faber & Faber, Ltd., 1963), chapter 6.

6. For anthropologically "primitive" conditions necessary for the emergence of politics, see Lucy Mair, *Primitive Government* (Baltimore: Penguin Books, 1962), Part 1.

7. Persistence is the main theme of David Easton's *A Systems Analysis of Political Life* (New York: John Wiley & Sons, Inc., 1965).

8. The expression "circumference" is also used by Kenneth Burke in a different context in his *A Grammar of Motives* (New York: Meridian Books, Inc., 1962), pp. 77ff.

9. Weber's definition of "political" can be found in *The Theory of Social and Economic Organization* (New York: The Free Press, 1947), p. 154.

10. Sartre's views on "The Republic of Silence," first stated in a French Resistance newspaper, are conveniently found in A. J. Liebling and Eugene Jay Sheffer, eds., *La République du Silence* (New York: Harcourt, Brace & World, Inc., 1946), pp. 442–445.

11. Erik H. Erikson, *Childhood and Society* (New York: W. W. Norton & Company, Inc., 1950), chapter 7.

12. Erikson, p. 225.

13. Erikson, p. 228.

14. Erikson, p. 225.

15. Erikson, p. 226.

16. Erikson, p. 226

17. Erikson, p. 228.

18. Erikson, p. 228.

19. On "basic trust," see Helen Merrell Lynd, *On Shame and The Search for Identity* (New York: Science Editions, 1961), p. 45.

20. ". . .we must accept it as a plain fact that many native 'citizens' have in no meaningful sense agreed to anything. They have never been asked and have never thought about it. They are political childbrides who have a status they do not understand and which they have not acquired by their own consent." Joseph Tussman, *Obligation and the Body Politic* (New York: Oxford University Press, 1960), pp. 36–37.

21. Erikson, "The Problem of Ego Identity," in Maurice R. Stein and Others, eds., *Identity and Anxiety, Survival of the Person in Mass Society* (New York: The Free Press, 1960), pp. 46–47. For an interesting attempt to relate job partici-

pation to personality development in modern work organizations, see Chris Argyris, *Personality and Organization, The Conflict between System and Individual* (New York: Harper & Row, Publishers, 1957).

22. Erikson, "The Problem of Ego Identity," pp. 46–47.

23. Erikson, "The Problem of Ego Identity," pp. 76–77.

24. Erikson, "The Problem of Ego Identity," p. 81.

25. Arthur Koestler's novel *Darkness at Noon* (1941) remains one of the classical studies in this problem.

26. See Philip Selznick's notion of the "stalinoid" personality in *The Organizational Weapon* (New York: McGraw-Hill, Inc., 1957), chapter 7.

27. Erikson, "The Problem of Ego Identity," pp. 84–85.

28. See Paul Goodman's comments on choices available for youth in modern society, *Growing Up Absurd* (New York: Vintage Books, 1960), *passim.* His views on "socialization" are found in his Introduction.

29. Erikson, "The Problem of Ego Identity," p. 85.

30. The work of Joseph Katz of the Institute for Human Problems at Stanford University, though published too late for inclusion in the main discussion of participation and identity, appears to corroborate the argument made in this essay. Surveying eight studies conducted on college activists, Katz notes that such students tend to be more intelligent, flexible, tolerant, and emotionally stable than nonactivists. At the same time, they tend to be less dependent upon authority. Yet while these activists are less dependent on authority, they have closer emotional and intellectual ties with their parents than do nonactivists. A composite study prepared for the U.S. Office of Education and reported in *The New York Times.* (June 19, 1967).

Index

Index